Transforming Play

Teaching Tactics
and
Game Sense

Dennis Slade

Human Kinetics

Library of Congress Cataloging-in-Publication Data

Slade, Dennis G.
    Transforming play : teaching tactics and game sense / Dennis G. Slade.
        p. cm.
    Includes bibliographical references.
    ISBN-13: 978-0-7360-7518-3 (soft cover)
    ISBN-10: 0-7360-7518-6 (soft cover)
    1. Sports–Study and teaching. 2. Teamwork (Sports)–Study and teaching. 3.
Group games–Study and teaching.   I. Title.
    GV361.S545   2009
    796.071–dc22

                                                                    2009025667

ISBN-10: 0-7360-7518-6 (print)
ISBN-13: 978-0-7360-7518-3 (print)

The Web addresses cited in this text were current as of August 2009, unless otherwise noted.

Acquisitions Editor: John Dickinson
Developmental Editor: Jacqueline Eaton Blakley
Assistant Editors: Lauren Morenz, Bethany J. Bentley, and Elizabeth Evans
Copyeditor: Patsy Fortney
Proofer: Jim Burns
Indexer: Bobbi Swanson
Permission Manager: Dalene Reeder
Graphic Designer: Fred Starbird
Graphic Artist: Angela K. Snyder
Cover Designer: Keith Blomberg
Photographer (cover): iStockphoto/Alberto Pomares
Art Manager: Kelly Hendren
Associate Art Manager: Alan L. Wilborn
Illustrator: Two Jay!
Printer: Versa Press

Printed in the United States of America

10   9   8   7   6   5   4   3   2   1

The paper in this book is certified under a sustainable forestry program.

Human Kinetics
Web site: www.HumanKinetics.com

United States: Human Kinetics
P.O. Box 5076
Champaign, IL 61825-5076
800-747-4457
e-mail: humank@hkusa.com

Canada: Human Kinetics
475 Devonshire Road Unit 100
Windsor, ON N8Y 2L5
800-465-7301 (in Canada only)
e-mail: info@hkcanada.com

Europe: Human Kinetics
107 Bradford Road
Stanningley
Leeds LS28 6AT, United Kingdom
+44 (0) 113 255 5665
e-mail: hk@hkeurope.com

Australia: Human Kinetics
57A Price Avenue
Lower Mitcham, South Australia 5062
08 8372 0999
e-mail: info@hkaustralia.com

New Zealand: Human Kinetics
P.O. Box 80
Torrens Park, South Australia 5062
0800 222 062
e-mail: info@hknewzealand.com

E4520

To the memory of George E. Slade and Rosina M. Slade, with respect for all that I learnt from them. To my wife, Philippa, and my children, Andrew, Richard and Caroline, for their unremitting encouragement and support.

Contents

3 Applying TGfU to Teaching Badminton, Basketball and Netball 87

4 Applying TGfU to Teaching Football 101

5 Authentic Assessment **115**

Introduction

As a child growing up in a small seaside town in New Zealand, I eagerly cycled home from school as fast as I could to play games with the community of kids of all ages and sizes in our immediate neighbourhood. The beauty of being home first was that you got to pick what game would be played—unless you were the smallest! Game contributions from my family were field hockey in the winter and cricket in the summer. Games from other families were football or rugby. One family had a badminton net; playing badminton with tennis rackets under the carport was great on wet days. One family that moved into the neighbourhood had a table tennis table and wooden bats, and this too quickly became a favourite game. There were also lots of cycling games including polo on cycles with a soccer ball as the chuck and hockey sticks as mallets. Because the street was a cul-de-sac and there were few cars, that particular game traversed the entire street!

Teams were chosen by a pick-up method. The two best players of the game (decided by general group consensus), starting about 2 metres apart, made alternate heel to toe foot placements, bringing them closer together. The player who was the last to be able to place his entire foot within the remaining space was the winner and had first pick. (Yes, we weren't particularly sensitive to issues of self-esteem; if you were good at the game, you were an early pick!) There were standard rules about what to do when the ball went over the fence or was lodged in gardens, but, with such a range of abilities, ages and experiences, game rules were always modified. For example, when we played rugby, our biggest players tackled the opposition's biggest players. If chance had it that a small player was left to tackle a big player, the unstated rule was that the big player did not knock the smaller one senseless! Only infrequently did smaller players ever stop bigger players— occasionally, the bigger player would fall over laughing at the smaller one's attempt, but no one ever got hurt beyond a bruise or a scratch.

We learned tactics through constant play and imitating older siblings or neighbours. If we mucked up, as we trudged back to restart the game, we were given advice—generally politely—on how to avoid making the same mistake next time. Team leaders or captains changed tactics based on who turned up to play. Occasionally, those tactics required rule changes if the rest of those playing thought the tactic unfair.

In our playing of games we never did drills. We never went for training runs. All games were self-umpired, and we seldom had cheats, though occasionally if players got too upset about some aspect of the game they would take their ball and go home! When that happened, the rest of us either sat down hoping they would come back or went home too. The games were competitive. We kept the score, and it was only darkness or being called home that ended the games. Importantly, we always came back the next day for more games.

Growing up and learning games within this community transformed our understanding of game tactics from a basic to a quite sophisticated level. Our techniques evolved because we were always playing and because the environment in which we played (a long, narrow lawn on two levels) required us to master techniques that would work well in that situation. Our understanding of game play was also transformed through the socialisation process of cooperative and relational play. We adapted how we played based on whose team we were in, the opposition and the game we were playing.

GAMES MODEL INSTRUCTION: THE TEACHING GAMES FOR UNDERSTANDING (TGFU) MODEL

My approach to game instruction in sport and physical education, especially for novices, is to try to capture aspects of the context of game learning I experienced as a young boy. I have found that non-specific games—games made up for teaching tactics or skill techniques or just because they are fun to play—very effectively achieve that outcome. I have also found that such games are also excellent ways to introduce novices to specific sports.

In a formal schooling context I believe that game model methodologies (e.g., the Bunker-Thorpe [1982] Teaching Games for Understanding [TGfU] model) and more recent derivatives of that model (e.g., Kirk and MacPhail's rethinking of the

Bunker-Thorpe method [2002] and Alan Launder's Play Practice model [2001]) provide templates for instruction that are able to replicate the game learning contexts I experienced as a child. My belief is supported by a growing worldwide acceptance in the literature of teaching games in this manner to the extent that Kirk noted: 'If we want students to learn to be good games players we must use TGfU or a comparable approach' (Kirk, cited in Griffin & Butler, 2005, p. 224).

The original TGfU model proposed by Bunker and Thorpe (1982), also encapsulated in the Kirk and MacPhail (2003) model shown in figure 1, advocated that novices start to learn games by actually playing them at their own level of competence and in a manner that promotes enjoyment, satisfaction and fun while they are learning. This approach to game instruction perhaps best addresses the inherent desire to play games and is a move away from a single skill-based teaching structure.

The motivation for Thorpe and Bunker to develop another approach to teaching games came from their dissatisfaction with the highly structured, teacher-directed, skill-based approach to teaching motor skills they observed in physical education classes. They did not believe that this method of game instruction provided a context of learning that represented the authentic nature of game learning, namely a combination of tactics and technique. The wide range of ability found in physical education classes meant that for some students the technique-based instruction was too easy and not necessary, while for others it was too difficult and they required more basic instruction especially focused on why you need to develop these techniques. They observed that either way both groups found the experience frustrating and unmotivating in terms of developing any desire to play games and sports.

Bunker and Thorpe believed that a superior approach to game instruction would be to allow students to play the game with basic tactics and techniques until the game broke down, and then, and only then, would teachers or coaches introduce additional skills to advance the players. Instead of developing skills in isolation from the game, this approach advocated setting out some very basic rules, getting the game going and providing specific motor skill instruction when students asked questions about techniques, for example 'How do you do that?' or 'How can you get the ball to travel that far?' This allowed students to play the games at various levels of ability

and interest. It certainly eliminated the 'When are we going to play the game?' plea from the class. Importantly, it recognised the seemingly inherent desire in children to play games.

In Bunker and Thorpe's TGfU model, instruction starts with a very basic, or modified, game and some clear rules adapted to the needs and level of the students. Games then develop; for some, games might not progress much beyond the introductory game, whereas for others, they could become very sophisticated adult versions of the sport. But game instruction is based on a continuum of student ability within the class, and the outcomes are honest and transparent. For example, within a class playing badminton the teacher might structure the instruction so that some students might be playing on half a court with a modified version of the game focusing on learning the basic play long or short strategy of the game. On other courts students might be playing the full adult version of doubles badminton.

The TGfU model advocates the following principles to enable students to discover tactics and, to a limited extent, techniques for themselves:

- **Game form.** Use a variety of games that encourage thought about the shape of the playing area and the fundamental problems associated with finding space when on attack and denying space when on defence. The adult version of the game is not necessary, but a close approximation is frequently developed.

- **Game appreciation.** Ensure that students know and understand the rules. Rules define the game and the tactics and strategies needed for successful play.

- **Tactical awareness.** Place students in situations that direct them to consider the tactics to be used in the game (e.g., creating and denying space, fast breaks, observing weaknesses in the opposition). For students to be able to observe and understand these concepts, you must have considerable skill in establishing the game and recognising the teaching moment of when to ask the right question. Pragmatically, games must be modified to reflect the learners' development so they can divide their attention between the primary task of executing technique and the secondary task of employing tactics.

- **Decision making.** Create opportunities for students to develop the anticipatory skills associated with when to attack, defend, or perhaps be patient and keep possession.

These outcomes are achieved by modifying the games. The modifications must ensure that all students, regardless of technical ability, can participate and make tactical decisions about how the game is played.

- **Skill execution.** Motor skills should be developed within the context of the game. Skills or techniques are taught in response to the individual's or the group's needs to achieve a desired outcome within a game. Motor skill learning is therefore driven by progress in the game; motor skills are not taught in isolated technique drills. Some students' skills may be immature versions of those executed in the adult game, but measured against the context of their development and the opposition, their skill level may still be acceptable.

- **Performance.** Performance is measured by the observed outcome of the previous processes against objective criteria that are independent of the learner. Is the student a good or bad player, school champion or international? Within the context of a physical education class, providing feedback to the learner on his performance should not necessarily be measured against some absolute standard of, for example, badminton performance but based on their previous experience and what progress he has made in understanding and playing the game. A less obvious but not less important measure for feedback to the student and to the teacher would be how much he appears to enjoy playing the game.

At all times the sequence of instruction (as set out in figure 1) requires starting the lessons with a modified game that, while reflecting the ability of the participants, also mirrors the basic strategies and tactics employed in the actual adult version of the game.

Using TGfU to Teach Techniques and Tactics

Some might argue that the ultimate outcome of motor skill learning is to reduce the level of mental processing needed to perform a skill at the automatic level. Skill repetition in the form of drills will achieve that outcome. Indeed, either through drills or games, the repeated successful and correct performance of a technique is necessary at some stage of learning to achieve automatic performance. Unfortunately, in games that are performed in open-skill environments, performance of the technique is only one part of the successful game equation.

To illustrate the importance of tactical knowledge in game play, I offer the following example from a rugby competition. In the Super 14 rugby competition played between elite teams from Australia, South Africa and New Zealand, I observed a match between a New Zealand (Hurricanes) and an Australian (Brumbies) team. In that match one of the Hurricanes' players, Ma'a Nonu (also a full New Zealand representative-All-Black), scored three tries. To score a try, one has to carry the ball and force it over the try line. In this match Ma'a Nonu's game statistics indicated that he had carried the ball for 120 metres (130 yd). For this player this would have meant no more than 30 seconds (if he ran slowly) with the ball in hand. Yet the game—and he played the full game—lasted for 80 minutes. So what did he do for the other 79 minutes and 30 seconds when he did not have the ball? Well, he obviously was involved in other techniques of the game, such as tackling, but he also constantly positioned himself and adjusted his position to assist to the defensive and offensive tactical plays of his team.

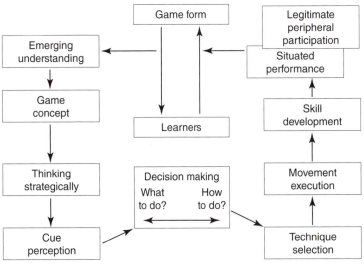

FIGURE 1 The Kirk and MacPhail TGfU model.

Reprinted, by permission, from D. Kirk and A. MacPhail, 2002, "Teaching games for understanding and situated learning: Rethinking the Bunker-Thorpe model," *Journal of Teaching in Physical Education* 21(2): 177-192.

Assisting tactically during the part of the game that took up 99 percent of Ma'a Nonu's playing time is not learned through drills of catching, throwing and running with the ball outside of a game environment. No matter how automatic his technique is, without an understanding of tactics, Ma'a Nonu's contribution to the game would be quite limited.

Learning the tactics of a game occurs best through playing the game (or modified scenarios of it) and receiving feedback on one's performance. Developing the performance of technique to the level of an automatic response enables players to better divide their concentration between the primary tasks (e.g., kicking the ball) and the secondary but more important tasks (e.g., kicking the ball appropriately to advance the score).

Helping players to know both how and when to perform a technique requires a methodology of instruction that does more than have them merely repeat technique in drill sessions. At an elite level understanding the tactics and strategies of the game is crucial to achieving success. This understanding is what often separates elite performers and teams of similar technical expertise.

The appeal of the TGfU approach for instructing novices in games is that the introduction requires the use of both techniques and decision making. It is the novice's desire to better affect the tactical outcome within the modified introductory game that provides them with the motivation to want to learn to develop their techniques.

Capturing the Learner's Interest

I have noticed in my own playing experiences that if I do not feel that I have made a contribution to the team, I do not usually enjoy the experience— regardless of whether my team wins or loses. When I do feel that I have made a contribution, I am eager to play again. To capture the interest of young players so that they want to play games and sports, you have to provide a context in which they feel that they contribute to the team performance. The TGfU, with its use of modified games and tactical approach, can provide an extremely positive introductory game learning experience for novices.

A study I conducted (Slade, 2007) that used a TGfU-designed field hockey programme (Slade, 2003) to introduce 58 novices to field hockey indicated quite conclusively that players perceived the TGfU approach as positive and motivating. Before the programme, students were asked whether they believed they would contribute to their teams' performance. Only 12 percent of the students predicted that they would. After the programme, the data indicated that 91 percent believed they had contributed to their teams' performance!

Work by Light (2003) and Light and Georgakis (2005) also supports the view that the TGfU approach captures student interest in playing games and can make them feel, even with minimal technical ability, that they have contributed to the team performance. Following the teaching of an undergraduate primary teacher trainee course on game instruction, Light (2003) and Light and Georgakis (2005) surveyed students on their impressions of the game sense methodology compared to their previous traditional experiences of learning games. Female respondents stated that they enjoyed the structure of the TGfU approach because any lack of technical ability was not exposed, and that they liked the inclusive nature of the games that involved everyone and not just the elite (Light & Georgakis, 2005, p. 72).

One student noted that learning games using a tactical approach meant that, although she was still not especially 'great at throwing or catching . . . she could still contribute strategically in defence or in attack'. The student continued, 'Learning basketball this way gave me a feeling of achievement and satisfaction that I have never experienced in sports' (Light, 2003, p. 98).

Another student from Light's (2003) study noted the following about learning games at school:

> I never knew what was going on or what I was supposed to do. I had no idea but here with the games we did I actually understood what was going on and felt like I actually contributed to the team, and that was enjoyable for a change. (Light, 2003, p. 99)

Transforming the Learner

In teaching games, you need to remember what motivates children to want to play games. Before children take part in formal games or sport, they experience play, which is the first building block of games and sports. For children play is mostly a social, fun experience that requires very little in the way of techniques. Playing games is another chance to be with friends and have fun, so you need to keep these motivating factors (play, fun and friendships) at the fore of any instruction.

The learning environment should give every student a chance to make meaningful contributions to team efforts.

© Ableimages/Riser/Getty Images

Transforming play into formal games and sports requires that students learn tactics and game sense, but the real transformation occurs within the students themselves. To transform students, you must create a learning environment in which they can make team contributions that they experience as legitimate and authentic. Having them play team games contributes to the creation of a social construction and transforms them from legitimate but peripheral novice participants to full members of the team, game or sport. Ensuring that the games have a tactical focus also increases students' tactical knowledge, allowing them to make tactical and legitimate contributions even without great expertise in the techniques of the game.

The approach to teaching games used in this text addresses the socialisation process of learning because games typically require cooperation. Even in individual sports such as singles tennis, players need to have a shared and accepted understanding of the rules and conventions of the game. Although the rules of tennis can be learned without even playing the game, the conventions—especially the moral dimensions such as calling opponents' shots in or out and the behaviour associated with on-court play—must be learned through participation within the community of tennis players.

Learning games and transforming learners is therefore as much about socialisation as it is about technique. Consequently, teaching games must start with playing games. Children demand it, as the following enjoinder that echoes in the gymnasiums and playing fields of all countries testifies: 'When can we have a game, Coach?'

When you use the TGfU model, ensure that the game is appropriate for the learners and that it emphasises both technique and social interaction (i.e., how one plays the game and all of its social nuances). By addressing all of the components of game play, not just the motor techniques, you offer all of your students—not just those with the already developed physical attributes for games—the chance to become immersed in the lifelong community of those who play and enjoy games.

HOW TO USE THIS BOOK

Easy-to-use games that teach fundamental movement skills and basic tactical and strategic concepts are the heart of this book. The first two chapters offer detailed activities for technique development (chapter 1) and tactical learning (chapter 2). In these opening chapters I have avoided introducing specific sports. Even quite young children have ideas about how major sports should be played including the social and cultural components. The use of non-specific games is my attempt to wipe the slate clean of any prescribed views they might have about playing a game. This will help them construct their tactical and strategic knowledge based purely on the game's nature and merits and how they and the other players interact in playing them. Less detailed activity ideas based on the same TGfU concepts are given in chapters 3 and 4 to develop greater proficiency in sports. Chapter 5 offers valuable information about authentic assessment of students' progress in games. A more detailed description of the chapters follows.

- **Chapter 1** uses the TGfU approach to teach some of the generic fundamental movements found in games. Running, dodging, catching and throwing are used almost exclusively in these games. Suggestions are made for further practice of specific movements as well as expanding students' sport language vocabulary.

- **Chapter 2** uses the same TGfU approach to develop a more specific focus on game tactics and strategies such as man-to-man marking, zone defences and fast breaks. The various sections include brief introductions to and overviews of the tactics and strategies covered by the games.

- **Chapter 3** illustrates the potential of the TGfU model to promote game learning in the context of specific sports. Game fundamentals, tactics and basic game declarative knowledge are taught in the sports of badminton, basketball and netball. The chapter also addresses the potential of this model of learning to capture students' interest and motivate them to play sports.

- **Chapter 4** further illustrates the potential of the TGfU model to introduce novices to a major sport. It illustrates through a series of games how players who are still exhibiting immature techniques of the game can learn aspects of football's declarative knowledge and tactics. It also illustrates how the philosophy of the approach allows competitive participation among players with quite diverse ranges of playing ability.

- **Chapter 5** discusses and demonstrates how authentic assessment can be easily integrated into game sessions without disturbing—but rather, enhancing—both game sense and the playing experience.

A glossary on page 127 provides simple definitions of the sport-specific language used in this text. References used in the text, as well as further suggested reading, are listed on page 129.

The activities in this text are designed for upper primary, intermediate and junior secondary school children (ages 10 to 15 years). They can also, with some imagination, be easily adapted to older and adult-level sport teams.

It is important to develop learners' understanding of and performance in games in a progressive manner. The games and strategies taught in this text are arranged in incremental steps to reinforce that process. Where you start in the text will depend on the composition and experience of the group or class you are instructing. Chapter 1 might be a good place to start with younger students; the games in this and all chapters can contribute to students' tactical understanding of games. You can adapt the games to a specific sport once your students grasp the concepts, although this may be done more easily within a sport team context than within a general class environment such as a physical education class.

Activity Format

A lesson plan–type format is adopted in this text to provide explanations of the games or activities with an emphasis on the tactics or fundamental movements involved. Activities are illustrated with diagrams that clarify positions, paths and play (see key to diagrams in figure 2).

- **Introductory comments:** The comments provided before listing the learning outcomes of the game provide an overview of the intent or form of the game both in terms of movement fundamentals and tactical considerations. In some instances references are made to other games and how previously taught techniques and concepts might be reinforced in teaching the current game.

The TGfU model offers great potential to capture learners' interest and motivate them to play sports.

© Alistair McQueen/age fotostock

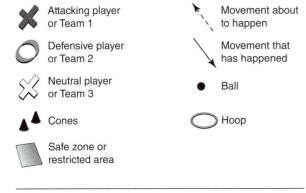

Attacking player or Team 1

Defensive player or Team 2

Neutral player or Team 3

Cones

Safe zone or restricted area

Movement about to happen

Movement that has happened

Ball

Hoop

FIGURE 2 Key to diagrams.

- **Learning objectives:** These are the specific learning outcomes of the game or activity.

- **Equipment:** This is a list of what is required to play the games. The list generally covers only what is required to play with one group, although in some instances it includes the equipment needed for large groups of learners.

- **Formation:** This provides the basic management instructions for assembling equipment and preparing the players for the games.

- **Recipe:** The recipe describes the game form and aspects of game appreciation referred to in the Bunker-Thorpe TGfU model. It provides a picture of how to conduct the game from both attacking and defensive perspectives.

- **Rules:** This section explains the basic playing conditions of the game that also contribute to the game's shape. Rules also give players an opportunity for critical reflection and decision making as they consider what they are and are not allowed to do. Where necessary, rules for both attackers and defenders are provided.

- **Variations:** These are progressions that you may use to challenge your students to more sophisticated understandings of the tactics, strategies and techniques used in the basic game.

- **Movement skills:** These are listed in the lesson plans for chapter 1 to reinforce the TGfU concept associated with skill execution.

- **Tactics and strategies:** This section provides a brief explanation of the tactics and strategies associated with the game. It highlights the decisions the players must make when playing the game and what they have to do to achieve those outcomes, and of course,

promotes questions about how to execute such techniques.

- **Attacking and defending skills:** This section places the learning outcomes in the context of the specific attacking or defending skills that are emphasised in the game.

- **Sport language:** This section lists terms players will be introduced to in the game. Membership of any community requires an understanding of the language of that group. Knowing specific sport language helps players share with other players an understanding of terms and outcomes, facilitates communication during games and brings players into the wider sphere of game players.

- **Questions and answers:** A key philosophical component to the TGfU approach to game instruction is constructivism. To construct their understanding of games, learners need to be asked how they thought things happened, what they might do next or how they should play in specific circumstances. The questions and answers provided are not exhaustive but guides to help teachers and coaches new to this approach to game instruction.

Using the Activities

The first step in using these activities is to have the students understand the rules and play the game. Next, introduce the questions that will lead the students towards considering the tactical implications associated with the game. Questioning is the key to achieving that outcome. Student responses will provide you with feedback on how successfully you are teaching the attacking and defensive concepts associated with the game. The questions and answers provided are not meant to represent an exhaustive list of what you could ask; they provide some direction and do relate to the tactical outcomes associated with each game.

You are responsible for deciding the time to allow for an activity, where you see it leading and how to integrate it with other games of a similar nature or specific team games that you are targeting.

Not all students will enthusiastically embrace this approach to teaching or grasp the concepts immediately. This process takes time, and some students will take quite a while to see beyond merely playing an enjoyable game. However, you could do much worse than provide an enjoyable game in a physical education lesson.

Elimination

In some of the games in this text, players are eliminated from play for various reasons. In most sport activities, being eliminated is counter-productive to learning the skill. However, in these games, the design is that those eliminated provide valuable data and feedback to other players, which helps to develop their own and others' understanding of the concepts associated with attack and defence. Eliminated players also provide the score, suggest goals for improvement and reinforce ideas such as cooperation and sacrificing one's own chance to score for the good of the team. This might be compared with a sacrifice bunt in softball, in which the batter deliberately sacrifices a chance to get onto a base to advance a player already on a base. Note also that in all of these games those eliminated are not excluded from the game for any extended period of time.

Playing Areas

Netball courts are a very useful playing area because they are divided into thirds (see figure 3). The thirds can be used to reinforce the concept of defensive, midfield and attacking zones. They also provide three mini-fields across the courts for younger players. Most schools have more than one netball court, which allows games to be set up at either end, leaving the middle third free for instruction, observation and equipment. The use of low cones down the middle of the court quickly provides six grids.

Outdoors, a grid system marked out on grass is extremely useful (see figure 4). Indoors, volleyball or badminton courts provide ideal playing areas.

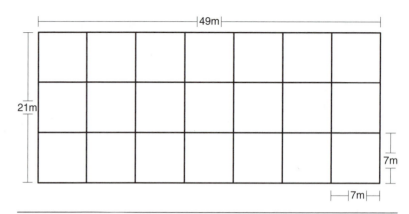

FIGURE 4   Grid.

SUMMARY

I hope you enjoy as much as I do the experience of teaching games using game model instruction methodologies, especially the TGfU model. Judging by the level of enthusiastic responses and happy faces exhibited by the students I've instructed in this manner, they certainly enjoy and learn from the experience. I suggest that in teaching these games you first establish the games and have the students play them, at least to a rudimentary level, before you require them to apply tactics and strategies associated with attack and defence in team games.

Remember, too, in teaching tactics, that questioning is the key to taking these activities to a level beyond that of just a game. Enjoy!

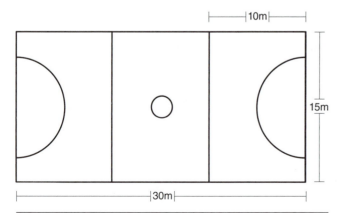

FIGURE 3   Netball court.

1

Fundamental Movements and Tactics

One of the great joys of playing a game or sport is implementing a tactic or strategy that results in one's team winning the contest. Talking about and devising such tactics, though, are often thought to be the preserve of the elite player or coach. Many believe that novices do not have sufficient technical skill to divide their attention between executing the technique and applying the tactic. This text turns that view on its head.

Using games that require only four fundamental movement skills—running, dodging, catching and throwing—and consequently minimal attention from the players towards technical skills, you can teach players generic game tactics.

This chapter teaches fundamental movements within a tactical game environment. It also provides suggestions for further practice of specific movements while expanding students' sport language vocabulary.

The Great Escape

This game dates back to the time children first played tag games. The simple objective is for defenders to chase and tag attackers. It is the first game in this text not because it is so simple or so old in concept, but because it allows you to introduce various terms and concepts that will be used throughout the text. For example, those doing the chasing are defenders and those avoiding capture are the attackers. The questions about the game introduce concepts such as finding space, or playing wide, on attack and congestion on defence.

Learning Objectives

Players will do the following:

- Chase
- Dodge
- Change pace while running
- Swerve
- Maintain space
- Congest space
- Double-team

Equipment

Three bibs

Formation

Use a netball court or similar-size area divided into thirds. Three easily identified defenders wear bibs, and the rest of the players act as attackers. All start inside the playing area that is divided into thirds. Players must stay inside the playing area unless they are tagged. Tagged players are out and must retreat to the nearest boundary line.

Recipe

Three defenders are chosen and required to wear bibs. The attacking players disperse anywhere inside the full playing area. On a start command (e.g., whistle), the defensive players enter the playing area and have a set time (e.g., 15 seconds) to tag as many of the attacking players as possible (figure a). Attacking players who are tagged are out and move

to the nearest boundary. At the end of the allotted time, the tagged players are counted, and that total represents the defenders' score.

After a short rest, with all players back in, the game is repeated, but play is confined to two thirds of the court (figure b). Tagged players are again counted as the defenders' score.

After another rest of sufficient duration for the three defenders (chasers) to have recovered, the game is played for a third time within the confines of one third of the playing area (figure c).

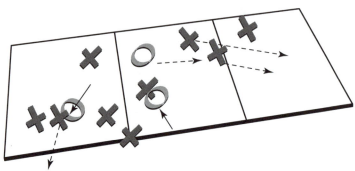

a Basic formation.

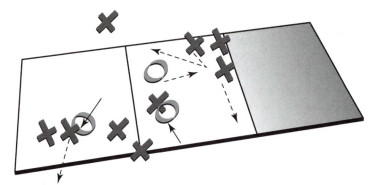

b It becomes easier to tag players when space restrictions are enforced.

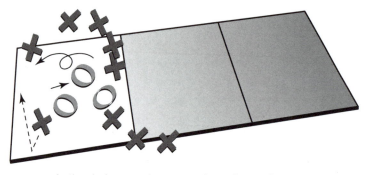

c As the playing area decreases, players have to become more inventive with their escape methods.

▸ Rules

- A player who is tagged is out. The number of players out represents the defenders' score.
- Attackers are confined to the defined playing area. An attacker who runs out of the playing area to avoid a chasing defender is deemed tagged and is out.
- Tagged-out players rejoin the game as soon as the set time is completed (e.g., 15 to 20 seconds).
- Tripping and hard pushes are not allowed.

▸ Variations

The class can be divided in half. One half of the class are called Team A and the other Team B. Team A moves into the playing area, and three players from team B become the chasers. After each 15-second period, the score is noted and, as the area shrinks, all members of team A are back in the game and three different chasers from team B chase. At the end of the game, team B has a combined score made up of those tagged in the three areas. The teams now change places. The only difference in this variation to the first version of the game is that instead of having, say, 27 players escaping from 3, the game is made more competitive and more people are involved.

▸ Sport Language

- Accelerating
- Swerving
- Space
- Congestion

▸ Movement Skills

Players may need additional practice in some of these techniques:

- Running and stopping quickly
- Dodging
- Changing pace while running
- Swerving

▸ Tactics and Strategies

The type of movement required by the attackers to avoid being tagged changes as the play area is restricted. Continuous movements are replaced by sharper, stop-start dodging movements.

Double-teaming: The defenders can coordinate their chasing so that two of them converge on one opponent, blocking his exit—double-teaming him to

effect a tag. If the defenders work as a team, they can herd players towards each other to increase their chances of making tags.

The progressions of the game should result in more players being tagged. Players should be able to identify the condition in the first game that allowed attackers to relatively easily avoid being tagged (i.e., more space). Try to get the players to answer the questions provided and also develop tactics to improve their scores. With junior classes this type of game can be played at very short notice; teach by commenting on the tactics you see the players using.

▸ Attacking Skills

- Running at varying speeds (speeding up and slowing down)
- Dodging
- Swerving while running
- Changing direction and accelerating quickly
- Using available space to stay as far from team-mates as possible

▸ Defending Skills

- Developing a plan for tagging as many players as possible
- Working together (i.e., double-teaming)
- Congesting the attackers' space

▸ Questions

General

Q: In what way does the game change in the three variations?

A: The playing area is progressively reduced.

Attackers

Q: When is attacking easiest in this game?

A: When there is plenty of space to dodge in relative to the number of defenders.

Q: Did the way the attackers moved to avoid being tagged change as the playing area became smaller?

A: Yes. They used shorter, faster and more sudden movements (dodging).

Defenders

Q: When is defending easiest in this game?

A: When the space is restricted for the attackers.

Q: Are there any tactics defenders could adopt to increase the number of successful tags?

A: Yes. They could coordinate the tagging by working together as a team.

Block Buster

This game follows a very simple concept—avoid being tagged! What shifts this game from a basic chase game such as The Great Escape to one with specific tactical learning outcomes is the addition of blockers. The blockers perform a function seen in games such as basketball, in which a player blocks, or screens, the opposing player from getting to the attacker, who momentarily gets free to perform some attacking option.

Children will recognise the chase and escape components, but it may take a little while for them to understand the blocking, or screening, function. Be patient and, initially at least, do not allow the players to run. Conducting the game at walking speed produces similar outcomes but reduces the likelihood of injuries. With older students this game would be a wonderful introduction to the screening concept found in basketball or many man-to-man marking scenarios in sports.

The tactical association with the name of the game is the chasers' object of trying to bust the blockers' screens and get to the attackers to tag them.

▶ Learning Objectives

Players will do the following:

- Coordinate chasing and tagging tactics
- Double-team
- Dodge
- Block and screen
- Use game communication skills

▶ Equipment

Two sets of 7 to 10 bibs (enough to divide your class into thirds and easily identify the three teams). If you have two games going, you would have six teams and need sufficient bibs to distinguish them.

▶ Formation

The ideal playing area is approximately 18 by 15 metres (about 20 by 16 yd), or one third of a netball court. Divide your group into three easily identified teams. Two teams start inside the defined area; the players on one team act as blockers while the players on the other team (attackers) attempt to avoid being tagged. The third team (defenders) is divided in half or into two groups of two or three players. Starting outside the area, each group of the chasing team takes a turn to chase by walking and trying to tag the attackers. The attacking team has two turns to avoid being tagged (against both halves of the defending team). Each team rotates through the three roles within the game. For safety reasons players in this game are restricted to walking.

▶ Recipe

Two teams (blockers and attackers) start in the defined playing area. Playing with their arms folded, the blockers provide blocks (screens) for the attackers to dodge behind to avoid being tagged. The blocking team may move (walk) or remain stationary. Their role in the game is to deliberately interpose themselves between the defenders (chasers) and the attackers. The attackers try to avoid being tagged for a period of time that you determine (e.g., 15 to 20 seconds). They do this by hiding and dodging around the blockers' blocks (screens). Because of the potential for collisions in this game, it is important for the teacher to establish fair-play rules and to closely monitor player attitudes to being blocked or colliding with someone.

The third team (defenders) is divided in half (with no more than three in a group) and starts outside of the defined area (figure a). Dividing the team gives those trying to avoid being tagged a better chance to do so. This forces the defenders (block busters) to coordinate their attacks because if they do not have a plan, they will find it difficult to tag anyone.

On the start signal, the defenders walk into the area and try to tag the attackers. Any player they tag moves out of the playing area as quickly as possible and without interfering with the game (figure b). At the end of the set time (15 to 20 seconds), the players not tagged are counted and that number is the attacking team's first score. This score is also allocated to the blocking team because the success of the attackers at avoiding tags is partly attributed to how well the blockers work.

After recording the score, the tagged players rejoin their team inside the defined area. After a short rest, the other half of the defending team has its turn at chasing and trying to tag the attackers (figure c).

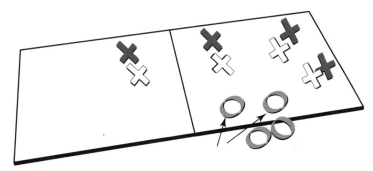

a

Basic formation.
Attackers can find cover behind blockers.

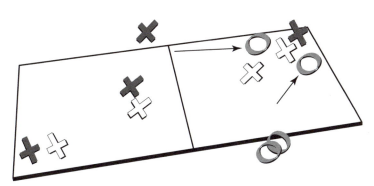

b

Defenders work together to tag opponents.

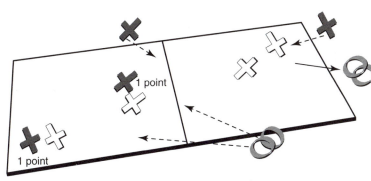

c

Attackers receive one point for every player remaining
once time is up. After this, the defending team is substituted
and the tagged attackers come back into play for another round.

Again, at the end of the playing time, the players not tagged (i.e., who are still in) are counted and the two scores are added to represent the attacking and blocking teams' score.

After the scores have been recorded, teams rotate their positions and play again. Table 1.1 shows a sample score sheet.

▶ Rules

- Players may only walk in this game.
- Blockers must keep their arms folded.
- Attackers are not allowed to hold on to blockers when they 'hide' behind them.
- When attackers are tagged, they are out and must move immediately to the side of the playing area.
- The number of players remaining in the game at the end of time represents the first score of the blockers and attackers playing at that time.
- Attackers who were out (tagged) rejoin the game when the second group of defenders comes in to tag.
- Discuss safety issues related to the surface of the playing area and especially the potential for players to be knocked over.

▶ Variations

Variations might include allowing players to move by jogging or running. Elite teams may use specific sports equipment (e.g., attackers and defenders dribble a basketball).

Table 1.1   Score Sheet for Block Buster

Draw	1 + 2v3		1 + 3v2		2 + 3v1		
Round	1a	1b	2a	2b	3a	3b	Totals
Team 1	4 + 3		1 + 3				11
Team 2	4 + 3				2 + 1		10
Team 3			1 + 3		2 + 1		7

Sport Language

- Blocking (screening)
- Double-teaming

Movement Skills

Players may need additional practice in some of these techniques:

- Walking with arms folded
- Walking and pivoting (rolling in the manner of 'off an upright pole' and then moving in another direction)

Tactics and Strategies

This is an extension of the game The Great Escape. However, with the playing space somewhat more congested and the blockers deliberately making the defenders' job difficult, the game requires decision making of a more complex type. In The Great Escape, players look after themselves, and so decision making is at a single stimulus response level. Decision making in this game is much more complex. The attackers and blockers need to coordinate their decisions about where and when to move. All players have to anticipate several other players' movements. To do so, they have to develop game communication skills, talking and body language and even discuss likely scenarios that they could employ to avoid being tagged. For example, the attackers need to use the blockers to force defenders to take indirect routes towards them. This increases the time the defenders take to catch them and so should increase their score.

To bust the blockers, defenders need to communicate and cooperate to double-team the attackers and channel them into isolated positions on the playing area so they can tag them. If the defenders do not work cooperatively, this becomes a very difficult task.

To be successful, all players have to remain alert for the duration of the game.

Attacking Skills

- Using a blocker to help avoid capture
- Intercepting or screening defenders

Defending Skills

- Communicating
- Coordinating chases
- Double-teaming

Questions

Attackers

Q: What is the best way to avoid having more than one person tagged at a time?

A: Spread out.

Q: What is the problem with being forced into corners?

A: There is usually only one exit, which makes it easier for the defender to anticipate escape actions.

Q: How can attackers use the blockers to avoid being tagged?

A: They can stay slightly behind the blocker to have the option of dodging from either side of the blocker to escape a tagger. They can also walk in close to a blocker so she can block or screen the path of a chasing defender.

Blockers

Q: What do blockers need to do to set successful blocks, or screens?

A: Anticipate defenders moving in on attackers and block their path.

A: Keep talking to the attackers because frequently it is difficult to see where they are.

Defenders

Q: What is the problem with chasing an attacker around a blocker?

A: The defender never catches up, and the blocker only has to move slightly to easily prevent the attempted tag.

Q: How can defenders trap players?

A: They can work in pairs to double-team, placing one player on each side of a blocker.

Q: How can defenders get the attackers to move towards them?

A: They can use one defender to chase the attackers into a corner while another guards the exits to try to cut down the chance of escape. In this example of teamwork, the waiting defender does the tagging.

Q: What is meant by the term *double-teaming*?

A: Using two people to tag one opponent.

Cone Down

This game provides opportunities to discuss cooperative game strategies from both attacking and defensive perspectives. Attackers learn tactics associated with width on attack, risk–cost benefits (playing the percentages) and the importance of pre-planning in games. Defending tactics focus on the importance of a compact, or contracted, defence. It introduces all players to game-specific communication skills. The game also develops the fundamental movements associated with running, dodging and agility.

▶ Learning Objectives

Players will do the following:

- Run in a congested area
- Perform agile movements associated with bending and dodging
- Feint attacks
- Calculate risk in both attacking and defensive roles
- Value cooperation in performing both attacking and defensive strategies
- Use game-specific communication skills

▶ Equipment

- One very large cone
- One hoop
- 20 to 30 medium-sized cones in two colours or types
- Bibs to distinguish teams

▶ Formation

Place the large single cone in the hoop in the middle of the playing area (a defined rectangular area such as two thirds of a netball or volleyball court). Place 10 to 15 cones of one colour about four or five steps out from and randomly around the large cone. Place the remaining 10 to 15 cones of the other colour or type outside of those cones closer to the boundaries of the playing area. The inner cones have a point value of 2, and the outer cones have a point value of 1.

Choose two teams of eight (team size will depend on class size). One team of eight is the attacking team. Players on this team arrange themselves around the perimeter of the playing area. The defending team places four players inside the playing area. The other four defensive players wait their turn to be defenders (figure a).

▶ Recipe

On a start command (e.g., whistle), the attacking team players enter the playing area and have 30 seconds to try to knock down or turn over **with their hands** as many of the cones as possible. At the end of 30 seconds the number of cones down and their respective values (2 or 1 point) are added up for a score out of 30 or 45 depending on the number of cones used (figure b). (*Note:* Attackers are not allowed to hold on to cones.) Table 1.2 shows a sample score sheet.

However, the attackers' main aim is to achieve 'cone down' by knocking down the single large cone in the hoop. 'Cone down' immediately stops the game, and the attackers receive an automatic score of 60 points.

The attackers are given five chances to attack, and their score is the total of the five attacks.

The defenders, only four at a time, defend the cones by tagging attacking players in the playing area. An attacker who is tagged must withdraw from the playing area before being allowed to immediately return to the game. Defenders can also stand up any cones knocked down.

Defenders must not hold on to cones and are not allowed to defend the large middle cone by standing inside the hoop around that cone. After each attack, the defenders must substitute at least two players. A player cannot defend more than two games in succession.

The cost benefit, or playing the percentages, is an important concept for both attackers and defenders in this game. For the attackers, the ultimate prize is to achieve 'cone down' and 60 points. However, the attackers must not focus solely on that outcome without ensuring that if that objective is not achieved, they have still knocked down lots of the other cones to ensure a good score.

For the defenders, the opposite applies. If they only focus on preventing a 'cone-down', then the attackers will still achieve very high scores against them—scores that they might not be able to match when it is their turn to be the attackers.

One final comment on 'selling' this game to young students is to suggest that when they are the attackers, it is a little like being a pirate and going on a raid for treasure, and for the defenders it is their job to repel the pirates and not let them get their treasure!

▸ Rules

Attackers

- Attackers may knock cones over only with their hands.
- Attackers may knock down only one cone at a time.
- Attackers may not hold on to a cone.
- No cones may be knocked down after the final whistle.
- Attackers may not touch the defenders.
- If tagged, attackers must immediately withdraw from the playing area and must not interfere with the game in any way. Once they have stepped outside of the playing area, they may rejoin the game.

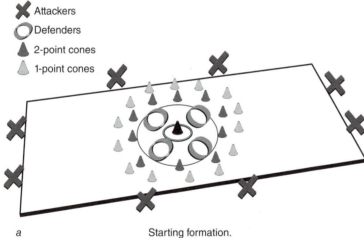

✕ Attackers
◯ Defenders
🔺 2-point cones
🔺 1-point cones

a   Starting formation.

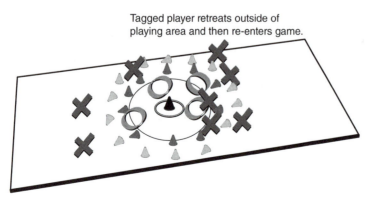

Tagged player retreats outside of playing area and then re-enters game.

b   Attackers can all come in at once.

- If the attacking team achieves 'cone down', the game stops.

Defenders

- Defenders may defend cones by tagging the attackers when they are inside the playing area.
- Defenders may stand up any cones that have been knocked down until the game ends.
- Defenders may not hold on to the cones.
- Defenders may not stand inside the hoop surrounding the main centre cone.

▸ Variations

- Variations in this game relate mainly to the numbers per team, the distance from the main cone that the other cones are placed and the number of defenders playing at any one time. It is important to give the attackers a numerical advantage; otherwise, there is little chance of achieving 'cone down'.
- A further variation is to have a larger defender-exclusive area around the main cone. Instead of a hoop, use skipping ropes to make a larger circle, or, inside a gymnasium, use the centre tip-off circle area marked out for basketball. The larger area will make achieving 'cone down' easier.

▸ Sport Language

- Agility
- Feinting
- Risk
- Playing the percentages
- Sacrificing
- Cover

▸ Movement Skills

Players may need additional practice in some of these techniques:

- Running and stopping quickly
- Dodging
- Agility (bending and picking up objects quickly while moving in various directions)
- Eye–hand coordination associated with dodging and knocking down cones

Tactics and Strategies

This extremely simple game provides tactical options for both attackers and defenders. The attackers have to divide their attention between getting as many cones down as possible and looking for a chance to achieve 'cone down'. They have to tempt defenders into standing up the cones or responding to attacks from one side while other members of their team attack from the other side.

Defenders have to coordinate their defence between not allowing all of the cones to be knocked down (resulting in opponents getting a large score) and defending the large cone.

This game at a very basic level introduces concepts associated with width on attack and compact defence and cover. It also introduces options associated with risk, playing the percentages and sacrificing players for other positive outcomes. An example is a sacrifice bunt in softball, in which the batter deliberately hits the ball in a direction that results in a high probability of their going out of the game so as to advance a player already on base.

This game can be played with very little instruction, especially as a warm-up activity. However, by assigning teams and encouraging teamwork such as developing attacking and defensive tactics, you change the potential outcomes for the game. Under those conditions, communicating and coordinating the attack and defence become very important skills. Teams should discuss such tactics before they start playing. The simplicity of the game allows quite young players to play while considering the tactics.

Attacking Skills

- Making quick changes of direction (agility)
- Feinting (i.e., making false attacks or drawing out the defenders to allow attacks from another direction)
- Coordinating attacks as a team and sacrificing attackers to achieve 'cone down'
- Having breadth in their attacks

Defending Skills

- Recognising opponents' likely attacking options and ploys
- Calculating the risk associated with tagging and standing up cones and also preventing 'cone down'
- Discussing defensive tactics

Questions

Attackers

Q: Is it better to spread players around the playing area or to all start in the same place?

A: It is better to spread out. Spreading out and attacking from different sides stretches the defensive resources of the opposition. In so doing, attackers make them play with their backs to each other so they cannot see all of the attacking options.

Table 1.2   Score Sheet for Cone Down

Attack	1-point cones	2-point cones	Cone Down 60 points	Individual attack scores
1	9	5 (10)		19
2	8	6 (12)		20
3	–	–	60	60
4	10	7 (14)		24
5	10	5 (10)		20
Totals	37	46	60	143
			Total	143

Q: How might the attacking team sacrifice players to try to secure a 'cone down'?

A: By directing an attack against the higher-scoring inner cones, attackers try to tempt the defenders to go for a defensive tag and provide an opportunity for a player to knock over the centre cone.

Q: Near the end of the attack time (30 seconds), what must attackers do?

A: While still looking for the 'cone-down' option, attackers also have to take the easy point-scoring opportunities of knocking down as many cones as possible (i.e., play the percentages) so that even if they don't get the ultimate prize, they still collect a good score.

Q: How can attackers keep the defenders from preventing them from knocking over the outer cones and not coming out to stand them up?

A: Attackers could keep one or two players in an attacking position near the centre cone so the defenders will not risk moving out to defend those outer cones.

Defenders

Q: How can defenders defend against attacks from all sides?

A: They can give players specific areas to mark.

Q: How do defenders overcome not being able to see all of the playing area?

A: They can talk to each other.

Q: How can defenders get in a position to stand up cones?

A: They can use cover from other defenders. They can also make tags and stand up whatever cones they can until their cover player calls them back into a tighter defensive position.

One Bounce

The next two games in sequence provide opportunities to discuss net game strategies— specifically, the attacking and defensive tactics of playing long and short. They also invite discussions on how to shorten an opponent's time to play the ball or how to defend by increasing the time it takes for the opponent to receive the ball (e.g., forcing an opponent wide). This game provides for further development of the fundamental movements associated with chest bounce passing and catching, anticipatory skills relating to angles found in net games and disguising passes.

▶ Learning Objectives

Players will do the following:

- Perform a two-handed bounce pass
- Catch a bounce pass
- Recognise passing and receiving angles
- Split jump
- Understand the tactical concepts of playing long and short in net games

▶ Equipment

- Four cones for every two or three players
- One ball (netball, volleyball, soccer ball or similar ball for every two or three players)

▶ Formation

Place the cones, two on top of each other, approximately 1.5 metres (1.6 yd) apart. If possible, place the cones on a marked line. Two players position themselves at least two steps back from and either side of the cones. One player, the server, has the ball. The third player stands in line with the cones and acts as the umpire and scorer.

▶ Recipe

The server starts the game by chest bounce passing the ball on his side of the line between the two cones to an opponent (figure a). Passes must be made with two hands on the ball, in line with and between the passer's waist and shoulders.

The receiver, on catching the ball, passes the ball back using the same chest bounce pass technique, ensuring that the ball bounces on his side of the line between and within the angles made by the position

of the cones (figure b). The pass must be made from where the player caught the ball. He cannot adjust his position after he has caught the ball. Not allowing that adjustment until after he has returned the ball is an extremely important part of this game. By bouncing the ball in a manner that makes an opponent move away from being directly in front of the cones, he is forced to return the ball from an acute angle (figure c). Because the rule does not allow the receiver to adjust his position before returning the ball, the angle of return is predictable and allows the other player to recover to a position that provides him with an advantage for the next pass. This is a basic strategy in almost all net games.

The objective of the game after first bouncing the ball on one's own side of the line is to also get the ball to bounce on the opponent's side of the line between the angles made by the cones.

Play is continuous until a point is scored. Points are scored when a ball bounces on the opponent's side of the cones, the opponent drops the ball, the opponent cannot return the ball with a one-bounce pass or the opponent's return does not pass through the angle made by the placement of the cones. You can determine the play-up to score (i.e., the winner is the first person to score 3, 5 or 7 points). A third player, acting as the umpire scorer, rotates in at the completion of a game.

▶ Rules

- At all starts and restarts (i.e., after points are scored), both players must retreat two or three steps back from the line between the cones.
- All passes must be two-handed bounce passes using the chest pass technique.
- Players cannot adjust their positions once they have received the ball.
- Players may pass as firmly or as softly as they please.
- Players alternate serves regardless of who wins the point.

▶ Variations

The second cones (note that two cones are placed on top of each other) can be removed and placed either inside or outside of the original cone placement

a   Starting formation.

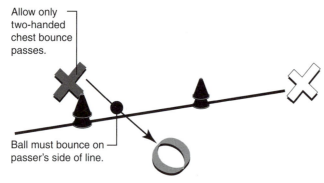

Allow only two-handed chest bounce passes.

Ball must bounce on passer's side of line.

b

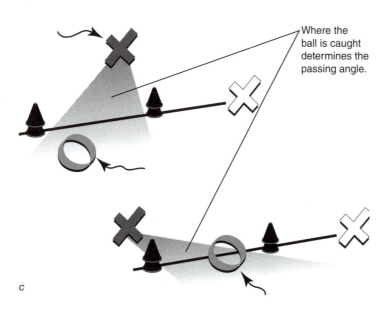

Where the ball is caught determines the passing angle.

c

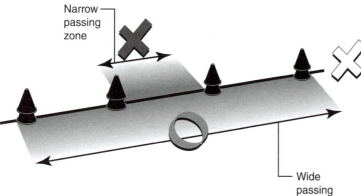

Narrow passing zone

Wide passing zone

d   Variation.

positions (figure *d*). In the second game, the winner of the first game plays between the narrower set of cones, and the losing player can bounce his passes between the wider cones, giving him a wider net or wider, easier angles to play through.

▸ Sport Language

- Passing angles
- Split jump
- Centre of gravity
- Stable position

▸ Movement Skills

Players may need additional instruction in the following:

- Fundamentals of the two-handed chest bounce pass
- The split jump: On observing the opponent's passing movement, the receiver employs a split astride jump and moves to get in line with the path of the ball.

▸ Tactics and Strategies

In many net or wall games, a tactic is to force the opponent as far from the net or wall as possible (playing long) before playing a short, or drop, shot (playing short). The same tactics can be adopted in this game. Wide passes also reduce the opponent's return bounce pass angle options and teach the receiver to move into the predicted angle of return. Also, if the pass forces the opponent wide and long, the receiver can move up to the line between the cones to anticipate the return in the manner of a tennis player coming to the net in anticipation of playing a volley to win the point.

Making the ball bounce high lengthens the time it takes the opponent to receive the ball and allows the player more recovery time. In many racquet games, the equivalent shot is the lob.

▸ Attacking Skills

- Disguising the direction of passes
- Disguising the force of passes (i.e., soft or hard)
- Taking advantage of wide-angled passes to move up to the line between the cones

Defending Skills

- Recognising opponents' likely attacking options
- Recovering from a pass (i.e., moving to a position that gives the best chance of receiving the opponent's next one-bounce pass)
- Using high-bouncing passes

Questions

Q: What is the advantage of a high-bounce pass to start the game?

A: It keeps the opponent back from the line or net.

A: A high-bounce pass increases the time it takes for the opponent to receive the ball and allows the passer time to adjust his position.

A: The further back from the cones the opponent receives the ball, the longer it takes the ball to get to the passer, allowing that player more time to get to the line or net.

Q: What is a long and short playing strategy?

A: Alternating between forcing the player back (long) and then bringing him forward (short). Typically, players play long before playing short.

Q: What is the advantage of performing the split jump?

A: It lowers the player's centre of gravity and provides a more stable balance point to apply force that takes him towards the path of the ball.

Crossbar Catch

This game has an interesting transfer effect from the previous game, One Bounce. In terms of tactics and strategies, the basic components of the two games, playing long and short, are the same. However, the fundamental skills required to play are different. This game requires the development of the two-handed underarm lob—and catching.

Learning Objectives

Players will do the following:

- Perform a two-handed underarm lob throw
- Use split jump footwork
- Catch a lobbed pass
- Recognise passing and receiving angles
- Use the attacking and defensive tactics of playing short and long

Equipment

- Two base stands and two uprights that can be placed securely in the stands and a crossbar that can be attached between the uprights (figure a)
- One ball (netball, volleyball, football or similar) for every three players

Formation

Mark off an area of approximately 7 by 7 metres (or about 8 by 8 yd; adjust the size to suit the ages and skill levels of your players). If permanent boundary markings are not available, use cones to mark out the playing area. Indoors, badminton court markings are especially useful. On a badminton court you could adjust the height of the net according to the developmental characteristics of your players and identify a play-through area of the net with strips of newspaper. The ball must travel over the net between the newspaper boundaries (figure b).

Set up the crossbar structure (similar to a high jump bar set-up) in the middle of the playing area. Two players position themselves on either side of the crossbar in their half of the square. One player, the server, has the ball. The third player stands in line with the crossbar and acts as the umpire and scorer.

Recipe

At the start of the game, the two players start one step in from the outside boundary line. The server starts the game by using a two-handed underarm throw to throw the ball into the opponent's half. To be legitimate, all throws must pass over the crossbar and between the lines of the uprights. They must also be thrown with the underarm technique so that the ball is always projected upwards.

The receiver, on catching the ball, throws it back, also using the two-handed underarm technique. The return throw must be made from where the player caught the ball. The player cannot adjust her position after she has caught the ball. The object is to get the ball to land on the opponent's side of the crossbar. A receiver can make one fake throwing movement before returning the ball.

Play is continuous until a point is scored. Points are scored when a ball lands in the opponent's side of the crossbar, the opponent drops the ball, the opponent cannot return the ball over the crossbar between the uprights, a throw hits the uprights or crossbar or the opponent's return lands outside of the playing area. A ball landing on the line is deemed in, or good. You can determine the play-up to score (i.e., the winner is the first person to score 3, 5 or 7 points). The third player, acting as the umpire and scorer, rotates in at the completion of a game.

Rules

- At all starts and restarts (i.e., after points are scored), both players must retreat to the start position (i.e., one step in from the back outline of the playing area).
- Players alternate restart serves regardless of who wins the point.
- All passes must be two-handed underarm throws that initially travel upwards.
- Players cannot adjust their position once they have received the ball.
- Players may throw as firmly or as softly as they please.
- A ball bouncing on the line is in, or good.
- A ball that hits the uprights or crossbar is deemed out, and a point is given to the opponent.

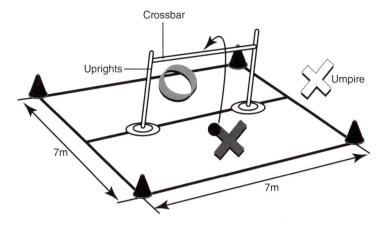

a   Starting formation.

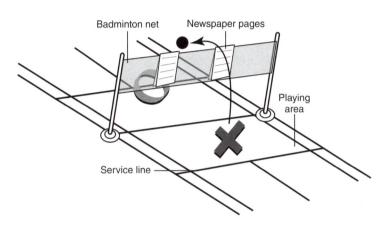

b   Alternative equipment.

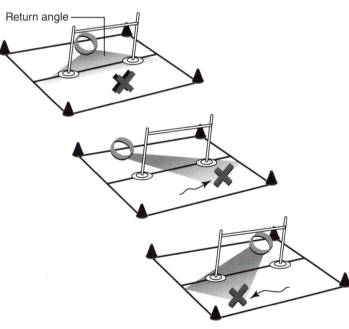

c   Where the ball is caught determines the opponent's return angle. Players learn to anticipate opponents' passing options.

›Variations

Teams of three play each other. The basic structure of the game remains the same (i.e., 1v1); however, the teams have to announce their playing order before the match. This could be done randomly or by order of seeding (i.e., the number one player on one team plays the opponents' number one player). Allow each team a 45-second time-out in any match for the other team-mates to provide feedback on tactics. Matches can be scored by accumulated matches or by totalling all points won.

›Sport Language

- Lob
- Disguise
- Fake

›Movement Skills

Players may need additional instruction in the following:

- Fundamentals of the two-handed underarm throw
- Catching a lobbed pass
- Recognising and then moving into the line of a throw
- Faking or disguising the direction of the throw
- The split jump: On observing the opponent's passing movement, the receiver employs a split astride jump and then quickly moves to get in line with the path of the ball.

›Tactics and Strategies

In many net and wall games, a tactic is to force the opponent as far from the net or wall as possible (playing long) before playing a short, or drop, shot (playing short). The same tactics can be adopted in this game (figure *c*). Wide passes also reduce the opponent's return throw angle options and teach the catcher to move into the predicted angle of return. Also, if the throw forces the opponent wide and long, the player can move up to the crossbar to anticipate the return in the manner of a tennis player hoping to play a volley and win the point.

▸ Attacking Skills

- Disguising the direction of throws
- Disguising the force of throws (soft or hard)
- Faking a throw
- Recognising the attacking opportunities of when to move in to the crossbar

▸ Defending Skills

- Recognising the opponent's likely attacking options
- Recovering to a position to allow the best chance of catching the opponent's next throw

▸ Questions

Q: What is the advantage of a high-lob throw to start the game?

A: It keeps the opponent back from the line or net.

A: It increases the time it takes for the opponent to receive the ball and allows the thrower time to adjust her position.

A: The further back from the bar or net the opponent passes the ball, the longer it takes to get it back, giving the player more time to get to the bar or net.

Q: What is the advantage of lower, quicker throws over high, slower lobs?

A: They speed up the game and increase the likelihood of the opponent making an error.

Q: What is the point of faking a throw?

A: To get the opponent to move away from the direction in which the player intends to throw the ball.

Team Play

Q: If players are put into teams (e.g., 3s), what are the options for you when deciding on the team playing order to play the opposition's team?

A: It can depend on the scoring system. If the overall team winner is decided by which team won the most games, then trying for even match-ups of ability might give you your best chance of success. If the team winner is decided by adding up the individual point scores in each game, then sometimes a mismatch can help you win. If one of your players can beat an opponent who does not score a point and the other players in your team, even if they lose the game, get close scores, you can still be the winning team.

Rotation Catch

The tactical focus of many net and court games is to place the ball into spaces in the opponents' territory as far from the opponents as possible. Placement is better still if it makes it difficult for opponents to return the ball. Playing this game well requires that players learn this tactic. In addition, the game provides opportunities for teaching the lateral movements, footwork and rotation techniques associated with the game of squash and with doubles net games, such as badminton and table tennis.

▶ Learning Objectives

Players will do the following:

- Catch and release (i.e., return a ball to an opponent very quickly)
- Disguise the direction of their throws
- Make quick lateral movements
- Coordinate their movements in and out of a playing zone with other team members
- Use movement-specific communication
- Recognise passing and receiving angles

▶ Equipment

One ball (netball, volleyball, soccer ball or similar) for every six players

▶ Formation

Use a badminton court and adjust the net according to the developmental characteristics of the players. If permanent boundary markings are not available, use cones to mark out the playing area. A minimum of three players are on each side. One player from each side starts just inside the playing area. One of these players has the ball and is the first person to serve and start the game. The other two players start behind this player just outside of the playing area. The three players from each side rotate in and out of the playing area in consecutive order.

▶ Recipe

The scoring, or playing, area for this game is the area on the badminton court immediately divided by the net. It is the area in the game of badminton that the shuttle must clear to be a legitimate serve (figure a). The server, positioned at the back of the playing area (the minimum badminton service line), starts the game by using a two-handed underarm throw into the opponents' half. The first two throws—the serve and return—must be thrown directly to the opposition players. This ensures that on the first two throws the learning outcome of having players rotate in and out of the playing area is achieved. To be legitimate, all throws must pass over the net, and on leaving the thrower's hand, the ball must always travel upwards. As soon the ball is thrown, the thrower moves laterally to allow his second player to enter the playing area.

The receiver, on catching the ball, throws it back, also using the two-handed underarm throwing technique. Return throws must be made from where the player catches the ball. The player cannot adjust his position after he has caught the ball. The object is to get the ball to land in the opponents' side. After throwing, the receiver moves immediately out of the playing area so the next team-mate may rotate in (figure b).

Throwers may disguise the direction of the pass (i.e., look one way and pass the other), but they are not to fake their throws (i.e., pretend to release the ball two or three times before actually throwing it). This is because in net games these types of fakes are not possible; disguising shots requires quite different techniques. The emphasis on quick return throws also helps players develop quick lateral court movements and requires them to time their movements in and out of the playing area. This type of understanding and communication between players is necessary in many court net games, especially badminton.

Play is continuous until a point is scored (figure c). Points are scored when a ball lands in the opponents' side, the opponents drop the ball, the opponents cannot return the ball over the net or the opponents' return lands outside of the playing area. A ball landing on the line is deemed in, or good. You can determine the play-up to score (i.e., the winner is the first team to score 3, 5 or 7 points).

It is important to have at least three players per team because two players do not get time to exit the playing area and both end up just staying in the play zone. This negates the learning outcome associated with teaching lateral movements, quick footwork and the timing of entries and exits.

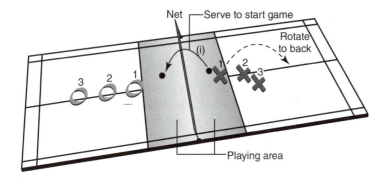

a

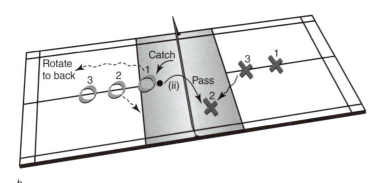

b

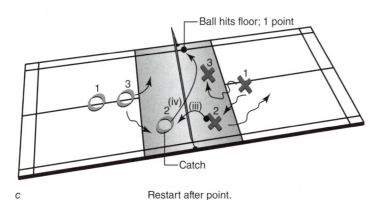

c

Restart after point.

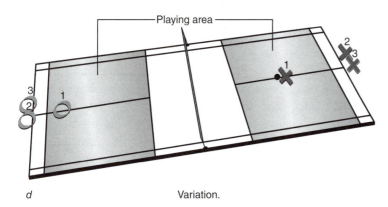

d

Variation.

- At all starts and restarts (i.e., after points are scored), all players must retreat to the start position (i.e., the baseline of the playing area).
- All passes must be two-handed underarm throws that initially travel upwards.
- Players cannot adjust their position once they have received the ball.
- Players cannot play the ball consecutively.
- Players may throw as firmly or as softly as they please.
- A ball that lands on the line is deemed in, or good.
- A ball touching the net or landing in the out zone is deemed out, and a point is awarded to the other team.
- Players must return passes immediately after they catch them and must not fake the return by pretending to pass the ball two or three times before releasing it.
- Players alternate serves regardless of who wins the point.
- Points are awarded for a ball landing in the opponents' playing area.
- The first serve and return are always easy passes directly to one's opponents.

Variation

The main variation in this game is to play in the area of the badminton court defined by the doubles serving area, which is behind the first line closest to the net, the widest sideline and the inside back boundary line of the badminton court (figure d). The objectives are the same, but the throwing distances are greater. The first version of the game develops players' soft touch close to the net and the second version, their more powerful game.

Sport Language

- Lob
- Disguise
- Rotation
- Lateral movement
- Communication

▸ Movement Skills

Players may need additional instruction in the following:

- Fundamentals of the two-handed underarm throw
- Catching and quickly releasing or throwing back
- Disguising the direction of the throw
- Lateral movements from a low crouching position requiring foot rotation in the intended direction, a side step and a turn while still maintaining a forward-looking stance

▸ Tactics and Strategies

The tactics of this game relate to the simple objective of putting the ball over the net into space in a way that will make it extremely difficult for the next opponent to catch and return the ball. Also, playing the ball to the place where the previous player is exiting can also cause confusion for the incoming player. In order to overcome this confusion and make it easy for the next player in the team to rotate into the playing area, if a player throws a ball to her left she should exit to her right. If she does that she will avoid moving into the next player's path of entry and prevent collisions. Players waiting for their turn to rotate into the game need to maintain concentration to anticipate both their entry into the passing sequence and the likely return passes from their opponents.

Players should try and achieve very fast catch and release movements. Competence in these movements puts pressure on opponents' rotation movements, making it difficult for them to keep up with the sequence of moving in and out of the playing area

Communication, or calling, is extremely important in this game.

▸ Attacking Skills

- Returning the ball away from opponents and into space
- Disguising the direction of throws
- Catching and very quickly returning the ball to the opponents
- Taking advantage of wide-angle throws to move up to the net to intercept return throws and speed up the game to a pace that prevents the incoming player from catching the ball

▸ Defending Skills

- Recognising opponents' likely attacking options
- Recovering to a position that allows the best chance of catching the opponents' next throw
- Moving out of the playing area quickly

▸ Questions

Q: What are the attacking pass options of a player who has the ball close to the net but almost on the sideline?

A: A short pass directly ahead or a long, narrow, angled pass along the net aimed to just clear the net and land on the opponents' side.

Q: What is a possible pass that will give a team that is struggling to get into position and has the ball time to get reorganised?

A: A high lob because it is the equivalent of playing a long ball and slows the game down.

Q: What must players do to ensure that they rotate smoothly in and out of the playing area?

A: They must quickly exit the area where the opponents are most likely to return the ball.

A: Recover quickly to re-enter the playing area.

Wall Ball

The attacking tactics in this game relate to the use of a rebound wall pass. This type of pass closely resembles the triangle pass used extensively in games such as field or ice hockey and football. The defensive tactics in the game are similar to many of those found in field positions in invasion games and specifically for goalkeepers in field hockey and football. In addition to those outcomes, the game provides further opportunities to develop players' footwork and the use of attacking and defensive angles found in net and wall games. This game transfers most directly to badminton, although elements of it transfer to wall games such as squash.

▶ Learning Objectives

Players will do the following:

- Roll a ball in an underarm fashion
- Field, or stop, a rolling ball
- Recognise potential passing and receiving angles

▶ Equipment

- One ball (volleyball, netball, soccer ball or similar) for every six players
- Two gym benches that act as walls for each court

▶ Formation

Place the benches parallel to the sides and position them equally in each half of a badminton or volleyball court. Three teams of two players result in six players per court. Two of the teams position themselves in pairs on each side of the court beyond the badminton minimum-distance service lines or behind the attack lines on a volleyball court (figure *a*). These players make up the attacking (passing) teams. Their objective is to pass the ball back and forth across the centre of the court. A successful pass through the centre of the court earns a point (figure *b*).

The other team of two players are the fielders. One of those players positions herself in the centre area of the court between the minimum badminton service lines or volleyball court attack lines. The objective for the fielders is to prevent the ball from passing through the centre of the court. The field-

ers can substitute for each other at their discretion but typically after they have saved a pass (figure *c*).

The benches act as rebound walls that the attackers can use to rebound their passes off to evade the midcourt defender. One of the passing teams has the ball and starts the game by attempting to roll it to the other team.

Games are played for 2 to 3 minutes with a 30-second discussion time-out after the first half of the game. At the end of time, passing teams record their scores, and the teams rotate. The game continues until each pair has played as the central defenders.

▶ Recipe

The server, positioned two steps in from the back of the court, starts the game by using a one-handed underarm throw, attempting to roll the ball along the floor past the single middle defender to the other attacking team. Depending on the age of the players, you may have to restrict how far forward the attackers (throwers) may come; however, they must not go into the defenders' area.

If the ball is not fielded in the centre area and passes through to the team at the other end of the court, a point is awarded to the attacking teams. The receiving team, on fielding the ball, rolls it back, also using a one-handed underarm technique. Throwers may disguise the direction of the pass (i.e., look one way and pass the other) or fake their throws (i.e., pretend to release the ball two or three times before they actually return it). The walls give players the chance to try to rebound the ball past the central defender.

Players cannot adjust their positions after they have fielded the ball, so generally, return throws are made from where the ball is fielded. One exception to this rule is that team-mates may pass the ball to each other before returning it to their opponents. However, such passes must not travel forward, so the player without the ball has to ensure that she is in line with or behind the player with the ball. In order to speed up this part of the game, these passes can be chest passes; they do not have to be rolled along the floor, but passes used to try and evade the centre defender must be rolled.

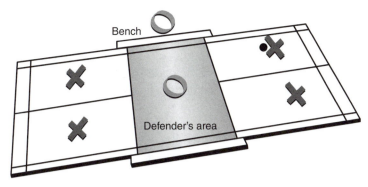

a Starting formation.

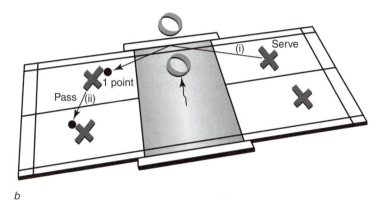

b

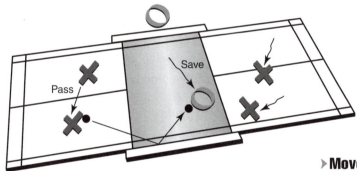

c

Rules

- Restarts occur when a central defender stops the ball. The ball is passed to the team that did not make the pass that was stopped. Restarts take place two steps in from the court baseline.
- All passes through the central defended area must be one-handed underarm rolls of the ball.
- Attacking players cannot adjust their positions once they have received the ball.
- Attacking players may pass the ball to each other before returning the ball, but the passes must not travel forward. This is the only time chest passes may be used.
- Central defenders may substitute for each other at any time in the game.

Variations

- Have two defenders in the middle zone.
- When fewer players are available, set up as in the manner of the game just described but without the middle fielders. Place a badminton net across the court at regulation height. In this version the objective is to roll the ball over the base or sidelines of the opponents' court not protected by the centre rebound walls. The net acts as a determiner of legitimate ball height. Any ball thrown that hits the net is illegitimate; players can either replay it or record a point for the opposition.
- This game can be played with football players and field hockey players using, respectively, either the side-foot pass in football or push passes used in field hockey.

Sport Language

- Disguising
- Narrowing angles
- Depth in defence
- Covering

Movement Skills

Players may need additional instruction in the following:

- Fundamentals of the one-handed underarm roll
- Disguising the direction of the one-handed underarm roll

Tactics and Strategies

The tactics of this game provide distinct learning experiences for both the attackers and defenders. Attackers can employ quick interpasses to make the defender adjust her position and provide gaps to pass through. They can also use the walls to create rebound angles to evade the defender. Disguising the direction of the pass is also an important movement skill to incorporate into the attackers' tactics.

For defenders, recognising and anticipating the possible passing and rebound angles are important tactical developments. They also have to use the central space to retreat to provide depth to their defensive tactics or to push up against a team to narrow its possible passing angles.

▸ Attacking Skills

- Fundamentals of the one-handed underarm roll of a ball
- Disguising the direction of the underarm roll of a ball
- Using the walls to make passing angles to evade the defender

▸ Defending Skills

- Recognising opponents' likely attacking options
- Recovering to a position to allow the best chance of fielding the opponents' next throw

▸ Questions

Attackers

Q: The defender is occupying the middle space of the court. What is an attacker's best passing option?

A: A wide-angled pass off the wall.

Q: The defender is occupying one side of the court as close to an attacker as possible, and the attacker is in line with her at the back of the court. What are the attacker's best passing options?

A: She can call her partner back or pass laterally back and forth to make the defender adjust her position. She could then use a straight pass when she believes the defender was unbalanced or out of time with the lateral passes.

Defenders

Q: The passers have the ball at the back of the court. What are the defensive options?

A:

- A defender could move towards the passer creating a 45-degree angle between her and the passer. That should ensure that the defender prevents the passing option on her side furthest from the passer. Having covered that pass, the defender can anticipate the direction, if not the timing, of her passing attempt. In addition, even if she passes the ball laterally to a partner, she can easily and quickly adjust her position by simply rotating towards the direction of the receiver, which would have the same defensive effect on the new passer.
- A second option is for the defender to retreat as far back in her playing area as possible. Because the passing team cannot bring the ball forward, whatever they decide as a passing option, the defender will have given herself the maximum amount of time possible to react to their pass before the ball reaches her.

Corner Ball

The attacking strategies associated with this game are sometimes referred to as off-ball attacking support and maintaining width in attack. Although the on-ball attacker (the player with the ball) is important, it is the off-ball attacking support players, who, anticipating the opponents' movements and getting into position in advance of the fleeing opponents, give the attacking team the opportunity to corner and tag opponents.

This game also builds on the dodging movements learned in previous games and combines them with the movement fundamentals of passing and catching but in congested areas. This shifts the emphasis from the technique of the throw to the quality of the decision making in terms of to whom to pass. Some player formations make this task relatively straightforward, especially spreading out (width on attack), but these formations require good teamwork to play well.

The main defensive tactic of the game is to anticipate the flow of the attackers' passes and to continually adjust one's position to avoid being cornered and tagged with the ball.

Learning Objectives

Players will do the following:

- Catch and throw a ball in congested space
- Provide off-ball attacking support
- Pivot and pass a ball
- Anticipate player movement
- Restrict players' movement direction options
- Communicate about specific tactical outcomes

Equipment

- One ball (netball, volleyball, soccer ball or similar) for every 12 players (*Note:* It is having two teams equal in number that is important and not the actual numbers in each team. However, six players per team is a good number in terms of ensuring all players get to experience all aspects of the game.)
- Enough bibs to distinguish the teams
- One hoop per game

Formation

Use a defined rectangular playing area to suit the numbers and developmental characteristics of the players (e.g., one third of a netball court, a volleyball court or part of a basketball court). If permanent boundary markings are not available, use cones to mark out the playing area. Create two equal teams of any number (e.g., seven). Teams line up in their half of the playing area. Halfway between the two teams, place the hoop (or similar target) outside of the playing area on the floor. One team member from each team stands beside the hoop, or target. One player from one of the teams stands in the middle of the playing area holding the ball.

Recipe

The game starts by the player holding the ball trying to score a bonus point and keep possession of the ball by successfully throwing or shooting the ball into the hoop. If the shot is successful, the team receives 1 bonus point and that team has the ball (figure *a*). The player from the scoring team who is waiting by the hoop retrieves the ball and throws it into the playing area to one of his team-mates (figure *b*). If the shot is not successful, possession of the ball goes to the other team.

Without running, but taking one step in any direction and using pivot actions with the ball, team members pass the ball among themselves to try to corner an opposing player and tag him with the ball (figure *c*). To be successful, the tagger must hold on to the ball while making the tag (i.e., the ball cannot be dropped during the tag process or thrown at the opponent). A tag is worth 2 points.

After a successful tag, teams return to the start position, and the person who made the tag attempts to throw the ball into the hoop for a bonus point and to maintain possession of the ball for his team.

Players must stay inside the playing area. A player stepping outside the playing area to avoid being tagged is deemed tagged. The game stops at that point, and players move back to the start position. Play is continuous until a player is cornered and a tag is made.

The opposition secures the ball if someone on the passing team drops the ball or throws it out of

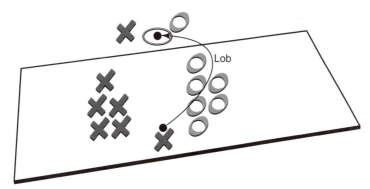

a   Starting formation.

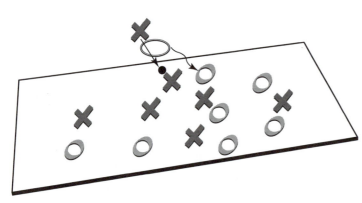

b   Team 2 players spread out and try to avoid being tagged.

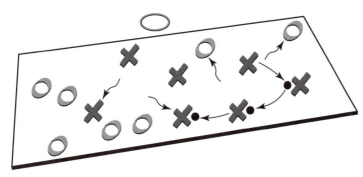

c   Team 1 uses pivot passes to chase, corner, and tag a Team 2 player.

bounds. The opposition cannot intercept the ball. If a member of the opposing team who is attempting to get out of the way is hit by a passed ball—not tagged—it is a turnover, and the opposition receives the ball. Restarts from turnovers take place directly from where the infringement or mistake took place (e.g., from where the ball was dropped). You can determine the play-up to score (i.e., the winner is the first team to score 3, 5 or 7 points).

▸ Rules

- At all starts and restarts (i.e., after points are scored), both teams return to the start position of being in two lines by the target
- Passes may be made with one or two hands.
- Passes cannot be intercepted.
- Players cannot run with the ball.
- Players can pivot with the ball (i.e., keep one foot grounded to the floor as they pivot, or swing step, with the other foot).
- A dropped ball or bounce pass results in a turnover.
- Teams earn 2 points for a tag and 1 for a successful shot at the hoop.
- When a player drops the ball while tagging, it is not a tag; rather, it is a turnover of possession to the other team.

▸ Variations

- Talking or calling to team-mates is not allowed. This encourages players to scan and look for passes rather than rely on verbal instructions. It also reduces the effect of players who constantly direct or dominant the game.
- You can specify various passing and catching techniques, such as catching with two hands and passing with one, or having players use a rugby ball and allowing only rugby-style side passes (i.e., no chest passes).

▸ Sport Language

- Closing down the players' options
- Pivoting
- On-ball attacker (player with the ball)
- Off-ball attacking support (an attacker without the ball who gets into position to support the attack as the opportunity arises)

▸ Movement Skills

Players may need additional instruction in the following:

- Fundamentals of the chest pass
- Catching
- Disguising the direction of the throw
- Pivoting

▶ Tactics and Strategies

The team with the ball needs to spread out and move the ball quickly to 'chase' players. Because players cannot run with the ball, they need to learn to catch, pivot and pass the ball very quickly. Other team members need to be constantly positioning themselves ahead of the ball to keep the ball moving towards the escaping opposition. This is equivalent to off-ball attacking support.

An effective tactic in this game is to target one player in the opposition to tag. Once he gets tired from running, he becomes an easy target. Although this is a legitimate tactic, it calls into question the spirit of fair play. I suggest not prompting teams to use this tactic. If they discover it on their own, it is a good opportunity to initiate a discussion of the spirit of fair play.

For the team without the ball, quick dodges and changes of direction are important evasive skills to develop. Players should try to avoid corners. When a player is caught between two players, neither of whom can quite reach him to effect a tag, the cornered player's best option is to dodge between them.

▶ Attacking Skills

- Quickly catching, pivoting and releasing the ball
- Positioning oneself ahead of the escaping players
- Anticipating where escaping players are moving to and passing ahead of them

▶ Defending Skills

- Changing direction with quick dodging movement
- Avoiding corners

▶ Questions

Q: What is a good attacking formation for the attacking team?

A: Spread the team out around the perimeter of the playing area so that passing options are always available ahead of the escaping players.

Q: Apart from passing ahead, what is a good tactic to catch and corner the opposition?

A: After passing in one direction several times, suddenly reverse the direction of the passes.

Q: Without calling for the ball, how can players indicate to team-mates that they are available to receive a pass?

A: They can have their hands up in front of them in a catching position and also use facial expressions to indicate that they are ready to receive a pass.

Q: What are some tactics for avoiding being tagged?

A: Players should try to avoid getting trapped in a corner, but if it happens, they should dodge between the two players. They can also frequently change direction.

Eliminator

The main attacking strategy associated with this game is known as the draw and pass. The tactic is common to many invasion games and requires the on-ball attacker to run at and draw the on-ball defender towards her. As the on-ball defender is committed to defending the on-ball attacker, a pass is made to an attacking on-ball support player, who receives the ball without a defender in front of her and is able to continue the attack unimpeded.

The main defensive tactic is to coordinate the defence to mark inside the running angle or line of the attackers and force them to move and pass in one direction. This defensive tactical ploy is sometimes referred to as a sliding zone defence.

This is the first game to require fundamental movements associated with catching and passing a ball while running and dodging. The restriction on the passing is that the pass must travel either laterally or backwards. These are quite complex skills, and players must be developmentally ready to undertake them.

▶ Learning Objectives

Players will do the following:

- Pass a ball laterally without it travelling forward
- Catch and pass a ball while running forward
- Use the skill of a draw and pass
- Coordinate their defence
- Use a sliding zone defence

▶ Equipment

- One rugby-type ball for every three players
- Six bibs to distinguish the defenders from the attackers

▶ Formation

Use a defined rectangular playing area such as a netball or basketball court. Three players wearing bibs are the designated defenders; the other three bibs are for the first three eliminated players to put on as they prepare to become the defenders. The defenders position themselves in the centre of the playing area. The rest of the class assembles at one end of the playing area in teams of three. One player per team of three is given a ball (figure *a*).

▶ Recipe

On the call of 'Start', all at the same time, the attacking teams of three move forward with the objective of evading the defenders and getting their ball to the opposite end of the playing area. They must do this without being tagged while in possession of the ball. To avoid this, they may run, dodge and pass the ball, but the ball must not travel forward. In addition, they are not allowed to drop the ball or run outside the playing area with the ball.

The defenders attempt to tag a player in possession of the ball, intercept a pass or pressure a player into throwing a poor pass that cannot be caught or is passed forward.

A player who is tagged, throws the poor pass, passes forward, drops the ball or runs outside of the playing area is eliminated. An eliminated player goes to one side of the playing area. Only one player per team may be eliminated in any one period of attack. On reaching the other end, attackers and defenders take up their respective positions and the attack starts again. Some teams will be reduced to two players or even, after several attacks, one player.

When any three players are eliminated, the game stops, and those three players become the new defending team and the defenders become an attacking unit. If more than three players are eliminated, the first three eliminated become the defending team. This is not the only way to choose new defending teams, but it avoids having players eliminated from the game for any extended period.

If the concept of allowing only lateral or back passes is new to the players, have them warm up for the game by jogging in teams of three, practising the technique. In the warm-up do not allow any opposition.

▶ Rules

- Players may run anywhere with the ball within the playing area.
- The ball can be passed only laterally or backwards. A forward pass results in the passer being eliminated.
- A player tagged while carrying the ball is eliminated.

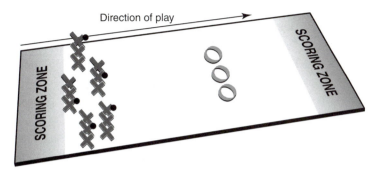

Direction of play

SCORING ZONE

SCORING ZONE

a   Starting formation.

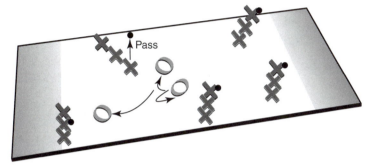

Pass

b   Defenders have not coordinated their defence.

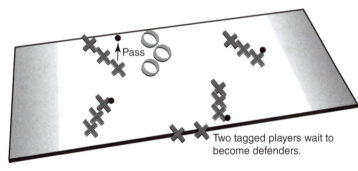

Pass

Two tagged players wait to become defenders.

c   Defenders target a team.

- A player who drops the ball or does not catch it is eliminated unless it is agreed that the pass was so poor it could not reasonably have been caught.
- When any three players are eliminated, they put on bibs and become the new defending team. The other teams are adjusted to ensure that each team has three players.

▸ Variations

- For classes new to the concept of the lateral pass while running forward, have only two defenders so attackers experience high levels of success.

- For classes more familiar with the concept, suggest a rule that requires the player who starts with the ball to also receive a pass before getting to the end of the playing area.

▸ Sport Language

- Draw and pass
- Sliding zone defence
- Zone defence
- Targeting a player
- On-ball attacker
- On-ball attacking support player
- On-ball defender
- On-ball defending support player

▸ Movement Skills

Players may need additional instruction in the following:

- Fundamentals of running and passing a ball laterally
- Running and catching a ball
- Dodging
- Drawing and passing

▸ Tactics and Strategies

For the attackers, the basic technique for avoiding the defenders is known as the draw and pass. The player with the ball targets and runs at one of the defenders drawing her towards her. This is known as the draw. At the last moment, before being tagged, the player passes the ball to a supporting player. The defender who has been drawn into a stationary position does not have time to turn and catch the player who receives the ball. There are many other passing manoeuvres that can be used or taught in this game, but the draw and pass is the most fundamental.

It is important that players learn the draw and pass and understand the cooperative strategies necessary to employ this evasive tactic. Conversely, the defenders will find making tags very difficult unless they work as a team and devise a defensive strategy.

To promote this type of strategic thinking for the attackers and defenders, have them play the game as described. After they have played it for a few trials, bring the teams together and get them to discuss attacking and defensive strategies. For the attackers, this typically requires ensuring that players run in support of each other. Defenders must learn to work as a team. If they focus on one team, they will have a better chance of making a tag (figures *b* and *c*). Their discussion should also include which team to target and the best way of doing that.

▶ Attacking Skills

- Drawing and passing
- Supporting running that allows a lateral pass

▶ Defending Skills

- Recognising opponents' likely attacking options
- Playing a zone defence
- Reading and anticipating likely passes
- Intercepting passes
- Disrupting receivers' passes
- Forcing teams to move in one direction
- Playing a sliding zone defence (i.e., marking on one side of a player and moving laterally across the playing area with her as she passes the ball, thus preventing her from bringing the ball back against the direction one is moving in)

▶ Questions

Attackers

Q: Why is it important for teams to stay together when attacking?

A: If the player with the ball runs away from her support players, she can be isolated by the defenders and will not be able to pass to a team-mate.

Q: Where should the support players run in relation to the ball carrier?

A: Two or three metres away and slightly behind the ball carrier so they can receive the ball without it being passed forward. Also note that by running in close support of the ball carrier, players can transfer the ball quickly giving defenders fewer interception opportunities.

Q: Where should the support player try to position herself in relation to the defenders?

A: In an overlap position (i.e., one in which they are not confronted by a defender). If she receives a pass, she should be able to run forward without immediate opposition.

Q: Why should the attacker delay passing when running directly at a defender?

A: By doing so, she draws the defender towards her, slowing her down so that when she passes, the defender has difficulty turning, chasing and catching the receiver.

Q: Do attackers always have to pass?

A: No. Players who create a pattern of always passing can be very successful with a random fake pass and a side step.

Defenders

Q: Should defenders try to tag players from several teams or target one team?

A: It is probably best to target one team. If defenders can make other tags, they should treat them as bonuses.

Q: How do defenders target a team?

A: The defenders decide to try to tag players within one team. They then align themselves in a way that forces that team to run and pass in only one direction. As the ball is passed across the team, the defenders continue to slide across inside of the receivers to the point that the last receiver does not have any passing options. In this situation the receiver is frequently tagged or forced to run out of the playing area.

Space Pass 1, 2 and 3

Space Pass is made up of three games in a hierarchical sequence; they progress from the relatively simple to the more complex. Each game is designed with the primary intention of teaching the players how to find space in games. Space Pass 1 is merely a pass, catch and move game. Space Pass 2 and 3, while still employing the movement fundamentals of catch, pass and move, identify specific areas players must strive to find while avoiding being marked by the opposition. This is done through the use of mats in the playing area.

At a tactical level the old adage 'it takes two to make a pass' accounts for success in these games. The passers must learn to read the intended directions of the receivers, where they want to receive the passes and the technique of completing accurate passes. The receivers need to develop their communication skills, calling and body language and the techniques of leading to receive the pass in space. Pass completions are not just down to the passer or the receiver; they require a coordination of minds, intents and techniques to achieve the desired outcomes. It takes two!

▶ Learning Objectives

Players will do the following:

- Catch, pass and move
- Make accurate passes in congested open-skill playing
- Move into empty space
- Lead to receive passes
- Use body language
- Mark opponents

▶ Equipment

- Six non-slip mats per game
- Volleyball, netball or similar ball (this game could easily be played with a rugby-type ball and used to teach, as a secondary outcome, rugby-style passes)
- Bibs to identify teams

▶ Formation

Choose a defined playing area large enough to allow movement for eight players. An area the size of one third of a netball court or a volleyball court is appropriate.

In all three games, two teams of four players occupy the playing area. One player starts with the ball from outside of the playing area. In Space Pass 2 and 3, six non-slip mats, or something similar, are distributed around the playing area. Players are not allowed to run with the ball.

▶ Recipe

Space Pass 1

The game starts with a player from one team passing, or throwing, the ball to a team-mate inside the playing area and then joining the game (figure a). Players cannot run with the ball but may move anywhere within the playing area. To score a point, a team must make four consecutive passes without dropping the ball, having it intercepted or throwing it outside of the playing area. After a point is scored, the ball is given to the opposing team, which restarts the game with a pass-in from outside the perimeter of the playing area. A dropped ball or other form of turnover (e.g., interception) results in play restarting from within the playing area as close to where the turnover occurred as possible. Note that in this first game of Space Pass 1, players are not allowed to make an immediate return pass to the player from whom they receive a pass.

You determine the play-up to score (i.e., the winning team is the first to score, for example, 3, 5 or 7 points).

Space Pass 2

In Space Pass 2, six mats (e.g., small gymnastic mats) are spaced evenly around the playing area (see figure b). There are two changes to this game from Space Pass 1. First, to score a point, players must catch four passes with at least one foot on one of the mats. However, if an opposition player also has his foot on the mat as the ball is received, then the catch is not recorded as one of the four needed to score a point. However, this does not result in a turnover of possession. The team retains possession and continues to pass the ball among the team-mates. Hence, in this game it may take many more than four consecutive passes to score a point. The second point of difference is that players may now make immediate return passes.

Players, both attacking and defending, may not wait on a mat for more than 3 seconds at a time. This puts pressure on the players to make decisions and is comparable to games such as netball, which allows a held possession for only 3 seconds, and basketball, which has a 3-second rule for remaining in the area immediately in front of the opponents' goal. If your players are quite young, you should adjust this rule to better reflect their developmental stage.

You determine the play-up to score (i.e., the winning team is the first to score, for example, 3, 5 or 7 points).

Space Pass 3

There is only one change in the game recipe between Space Pass 2 and 3. In Space Pass 3, players, neither the attackers nor defenders, are not allowed to wait on a mat to receive a pass or mark a player. This is an extremely important change because now the passer must make his throw so it passes over the mat at the same time that the receiver arrives (figure c). That is, he has to pass into space—hence the name of the game. This is an advanced level of instruction on leading, receiving and passing into space. This rule change also requires the marker to anticipate the receiver's movement and arrive at the mat at the same time as the receiver.

You determine the play-up to score (i.e., the winning team is the first to score, for example, 3, 5 or 7 points).

▸ Rules

- All starts and restarts (i.e., after points are scored) take place with a throw-in from a boundary line to a team member.
- There should be two more mats than players per team (4v4 requires six mats).
- No running with the ball.

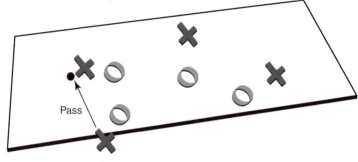

a   Space Pass 1.

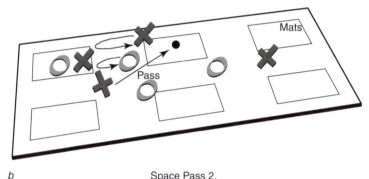

b   Space Pass 2.

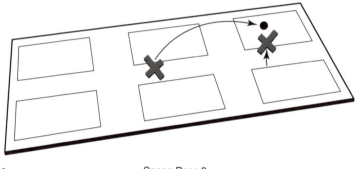

c   Space Pass 3.

- The ball can be bounce passed.
- Points are awarded for catching a ball on a mat as long as an opponent's foot is not also on the mat at the time of the catch.
- Turnovers result from dropped catches (including bounce passes), interceptions and if the ball is thrown out.
- All players must stay 1.5 metres (two steps) away from the person attempting to throw, or pass, the ball. A ball not taken cleanly (i.e., dropped) in an attempted interception remains in the possession of the passing team.

- The ball cannot be held without making a pass for more than 5 seconds.
- Players alternate restarts regardless of who wins the point.

▶ Variations

Variations to this game include changing the type of ball that is used and nominating the type of throws employed. If you want to focus on non-verbal communication outcomes, then do not allow players to call for passes or talk in defence. However, do allow time-outs for teams to discuss non-verbal communication strategies.

In explaining the non-verbal variation of the game, you could refer to the overload principle. Explain that you are forcing them to work only with visual feedback, that is, you are overloading this component of their decision-making skills. When they return to being able to use both visual and verbal communication skills, the game should be easier.

▶ Sport Language

- Leading
- Dodging
- Emptying the space
- Body language
- Scanning

▶ Movement Skills

Players may need additional instruction in the following:

- Fundamentals of catching, passing and moving into space
- Body language that indicates intended direction of a movement or pass
- Dodging

▶ Tactics and Strategies

Although spreading out when in possession is an obvious tactical ploy, the main tactical advantage in this game derives from the ability to lead into a space and onto a mat to receive a pass. For this movement to be successful, players should be taught to 'empty the space'. This term means to lead away from the intended direction—taking their markers with them. Hence, they are emptying the space of the opponent marker. Then, suddenly, they turn and lead back into the space and onto the mat using the unexpected turn to get away from the marker.

Communication (calling) is extremely important in this game. Depending on their developmental stage, players can also be taught to make subtle use of body language, eye contact and hand signals of intended direction while first faking and moving in the opposite direction. Also extremely important is the ability to scan and look for space and unoccupied mats to receive passes and score points.

Although the primary outcome of these two games is finding space, it also introduces man-to-man marking. Importantly, this very close marking is achieved without players having to have contact.

▶ Attacking Skills

- Accurate throwing and passing, especially judging the force and weight to apply to the ball
- Quickly catching and releasing the ball
- Using body language to indicate where you want the player to receive the pass
- Dodging
- Leading and dodging into space
- Scanning

▶ Defending Skills

- Recognising opponents' likely attacking options
- Marking players
- Protecting spaces (i.e., mats)
- Reading and anticipating likely passes
- Intercepting passes
- Disrupting receivers' passes

▶ Questions

Attackers

Q: What are three ways to get into space to receive a pass?

A: To get into space to receive a pass, a player can lead the marker away from the catching space before suddenly returning to the original position to receive the ball, lead directly to a passer or indicate that he wants to receive a pass in his hand on the side farthest away from the marker.

Q: What can receivers do to help the passer get the ball to them?

A: Individual receivers can make good use of body language. The team should discuss this as part of the game preparation so everyone knows the signals.

A: As a team, try to provide more than one passing option to the passer.

Q: What should an attacker do who is without the ball and not in a position to receive the next pass?

A: Move into a space that forces the defenders to consider marking him. This forces the opponents to spread their defence and makes passes to teammates easier for the person with the ball. In addition, the attacker can also scan to see a possible next pass if he does receive the ball.

Defenders

Q: Is there an attacker pass that defenders should allow?

A: In Space Pass 2 and 3, defenders should allow passes that they are unsure about intercepting but that they know do not allow attackers to reach out and place their foot on the mat and score a point.

Q: Where is a good place to stand to mark a player in this game?

A: Players should try to stay between the opponent and the mat or close to the mat so they can put their foot on it if they cannot intercept the pass.

Q: An attacker moves away from one of the mats. How should a defender mark him?

A: The defender should stay between the player and the mat but not rush after him, which could result in his being caught out by a sudden dodge back to the mat by the attacker.

Throw Golf

Throw Golf provides a game context that allows you to assess students' single-arm throwing techniques. In addition, it introduces students to the cost–benefit of playing the percentages tactics of golf, a game in which players frequently make decisions about whether to take high- or low-risk shots, which in this game, are throws. Finally, it introduces students to the subtleties of game etiquette for which the game of golf is famous.

▶ Learning Objectives

Players will do the following:

- Perform an overarm throw
- Improve the accuracy of their throwing
- Develop their kinesthetic awareness relative to weighting a throw to a target
- Make cost–benefit tactical game decisions
- Understand the concept of game etiquette

▶ Equipment

- One tennis ball per player
- Nine hoops and 27 cones (18 cones could be low cones to indicate the 'tee-off' area and 9 high, representing the 'flags' in the golf holes, the hoops)
- Score sheets with golf information (e.g., name and hole number, par for the hole)

▶ Formation

Choose a large playing area such as the school grounds or a park. Design a nine-hole golf course around the area. Use two small cones to indicate the 'tee-off' area and a hoop with a single large cone in it (the flag) as the hole (figure a). This must be completed in advance of playing the game. Divide your group by 9 to determine how many players start at each hole (e.g., 27 players would result in 3 players starting at each hole). This ensures that everyone is allocated a starting hole so all players start the game at the same time. Ensure that the players all have an overview or map of the layout of the course so they know where to move to after each hole. Players all start at the same time.

▶ Recipe

The game is played like golf except that players throw tennis balls around the course and into the holes rather than hitting golf balls with clubs. All the rules of golf, especially the etiquette of golf, applies to the game. Players start from a tee that is defined by two low cones and attempt to throw their tennis balls, in as few throws as possible, into the hole. A hoop with a cone placed on the ground inside of it indicates a hole.

A hole is completed when the tennis ball hits the cone inside the hoop or when it bounces or rolls into the hoop. The ball does not have to stay in the hoop. A ball that hits a hoop (not the ground inside it) and bounces away is deemed to be alive, and the hole is yet to be completed.

The course layout is left to your imagination. However, include holes that have par 3s, 4s and 5s. This ensures that the players need to use a variety of throws, varying from as hard as they can (par 5) to more delicately weighted efforts (par 3) to complete the course.

As in real golf courses, use the environment of your area to add fun and interest to the course (figures b and c). Play around the corners of buildings or over a fence. You might treat all footpaths within the area as water hazards. These hazards should incur penalties in the manner of the golf game. Ensure that there are risks built into the course. For example, throwing safely beside the tennis court fence or going over the fence in the knowledge that the tennis courts are an out-of-bounds area and if the attempted throw and shorter route to the hole is not successful and the ball lands on the tennis court, the player will incur a penalty. Teaching golf etiquette and language can add to the fun of this activity.

Collect the scores to help inform you of the throwing ability of your class. You can also observe technique. The game provides a diagnostic assessment for any throwing programme you may wish to implement. You can play the game again as a post-programme measure (summative assessment) of improvement in throwing or playing tactics.

▶ Rules

- All the usual golf rules apply plus any that you make up for your own course.
- Game etiquette: Other concepts could be discussed such as who plays first, playing through, not talking when someone is taking a shot and congratulating an opponent's good shot.

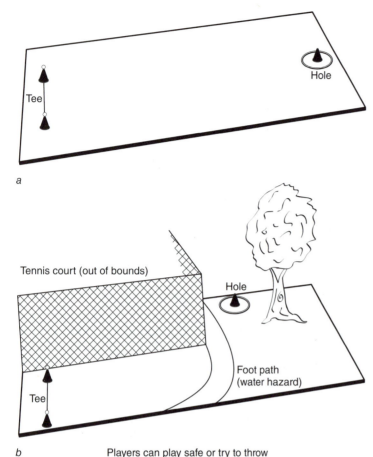

a

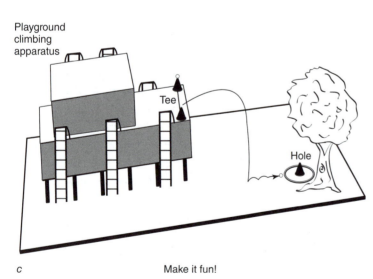

b

Players can play safe or try to throw over the edge of the tennis court.

c

Make it fun!

▶ Variations

All the golf variations are available. You could have stroke or match play, handicap or non-handicap games or team golf. You could introduce awards such as for the longest throw closest to the pin or, less conventionally, the luckiest throw! You could insist on

the ball remaining in the hoop or restrict the types of throws players can use. The same game can also be played with a Frisbee.

▶ Sport Language

Golf has a language all its own. However, you can cover some basics such as the following:

- Par
- Birdie
- Albatross
- Bogey
- Handicap
- Stroke play
- Match play

▶ Movement Skills

Players may need additional instruction in overarm throwing action.

▶ Tactics and Strategies

Tactics will arise out of the nature of the competitions you organise (e.g., stroke, match or team play). Most strategies in golf appear to relate to cost–benefit tactical game decisions. Does the risk justify the likely advantage or disadvantage of a successful or unsuccessful outcome?

▶ Attacking and Defending Skills

Attacking and defending skills seem to relate to the nature of the competition and minimising or maximising risk. In team competitions, players should discuss the tactic of one player playing high-risk shots while the other provides a safety backup approach.

▶ Questions

Q: In stroke or match play, when would a player employ higher-risk throws?

A: When she is trailing and a successful outcome of a high-risk shot is the only way she could possibly win the match. A successful outcome would force her opponent to also choose a high-risk shot, which is one that she might find difficult to achieve.

A: When she has little to lose if the shot or throw is unsuccessful—that is, a conservative shot will not help her score and she has run out of holes left to play to win if she does not go for it.

Q: When should players avoid high-risk shots?

A: When they are defending a lead.

A: When, in the relation to the state of the game, the risk–gain ratio is too high in favour of the risk.

Piltz Pass

The tactical focus of this game is on body language to indicate when players are available to receive a pass. The game requires the players to look up and scan the area for passes. Rule variations also teach players the importance of on-ball support play, especially when they are behind the attacking on-ball player. Rule variations also provide opportunities to discuss strategies for allowing players time to get forward in advance of the on-ball player to draw defenders away from the midfield of the game. It invites a discussion of the concept of developing attacks from deep within one's own defensive area.

In addition, this game combines some of the movement outcomes of previous games (e.g., finding and passing into space and back and around passes). The game also builds on some of the throwing techniques refined in the previous game, Throw Golf.

▶ Learning Objectives

Players will do the following:

- Throw and catch a small ball with a Velcro glove
- Throw accurately in an open-skill environment
- Lead and dodge back to receive passes
- Use body language to indicate their availability to receive a pass
- Use body language to indicate where they want the passer to throw the ball
- Look up and scan the playing area for possible passes
- Provide support play to the player with the ball

▶ Equipment

- Two sets of Velcro gloves; enough for one for each on-court player. The gloves should be in two distinctive colours to distinguish the teams. One team might have green Velcro gloves and the other team, red. If distinctive gloves cannot be found, then baseball or softball gloves can be used, but teams would then need to be distinguished by the use of bibs.

- One Velcro tennis ball that will stick to the glove when it hits it (see Variations for alternative equipment).
- As a variation, you could substitute the Velcro gloves for softball or baseball gloves and have players use a tennis ball. If you use this variation, you will need to identify the teams by having them wear bibs.

Note: The Velcro gloves can be purchased commercially along with the ball that will stick to it. It looks like a large saucer or discus with an adjustable strap on the back where the player puts his hand. The Velcro side of the glove is presented whenever a player shows the palm of his hand (in this way it acts like a baseball glove). The ball is a furry tennis ball and when it makes contact with the glove, it sticks to it, thus effecting a catch.

▶ Formation

Choose a defined playing area according to the numbers of players. Depending on numbers per team, a netball or basketball court works well with teams of six or seven on each side. One player from each team is the goal receiver, and he starts the match in the goal-receiving zone behind the opposition team. The other six players start in their own defensive half (figure *a*). The goal-receiving player is confined to the receiving zone but may move laterally across the width of the court to receive passes. Defensive players may shadow the goal-receiving player, but they are not allowed into the goal receiver's zone. Players on the same team must all wear the same-coloured Velcro catching glove.

▶ Recipe

The team starting with possession starts the game by passing the ball back from the centre of the court. The objective of the game is to score a goal by passing the ball from the attacking quarter to the goal receiver, who plays within a receiving zone behind the opponents' defensive half (figure *b*).

After a goal is scored, the person who made the pass to the goal receiver changes places with him

Adapted, by permission, from Wendy Piltz, University of South Australia. Piltz Pass is named after outstanding teacher Wendy Piltz (University of South Australia), who demonstrated the Velcro glove version of this game in a Play Practice Lacrosse presentation at a TGfU conference in Sydney in 2006.

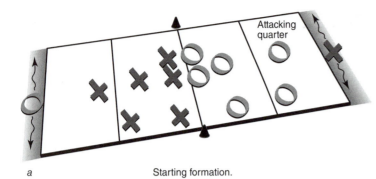

a   Starting formation.

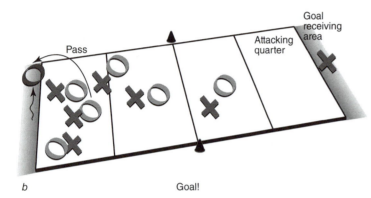

b   Goal!

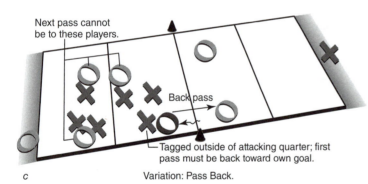

c   Variation: Pass Back.

and becomes the goal receiver. The former goal receiver joins the game as a field player. After a goal is scored, the attacking team must retreat out of the attacking quarter to allow the opposition a free pass to restart the game.

Players may only throw the ball with an underarm action (this is a safety restriction). Throws can be made in any direction and of any length. Players may also run with the ball and may pass the ball while running. To stop a player from running with the ball, an opposing player must be tagged. A tagged player must stop and return to the point of the tag and pass the ball. There are no limits to the number of tags a team may incur. All players, both attackers and defenders, must be at least two steps back from the player making a pass. After a tag, a player has 5 seconds to pass the ball or a turnover is declared. Turnovers occur if the ball is dropped, intercepted, thrown out or thrown beyond the goal receiver's zone. All restarts from turnovers take place at the point of infringement.

No talking is allowed during the game. Players may use body language (e.g., a wave or clap), but they may not verbally call out for a pass. Encourage players to turn their gloves towards the team-mate who has the ball so they can identify themselves by colour code. This also teaches the players forward of the passer to turn, look back and indicate by showing their gloves they are available for a pass.

You determine the play-up to score (i.e., the winning team is the first to score 3, 5 or 7 points).

If using Velcro gloves is a new activity for the class, you might consider the following as a brief warm-up and familiarisation activity for the class. Have players practise throwing and catching in twos or threes. Make it a requirement that the receiver must be moving when he catches the ball and that he must be showing the thrower the coloured side of his glove. Encourage dodging movements in this activity (i.e., quick, short dodges towards or away from the thrower) or running a V (i.e., starting with a movement towards the thrower and then dodging away to receive the pass). Invert the V dodging and receiving drill.

▶ **Rules**

- Players **may not talk** or make verbal calls of any kind for the ball.
- Players may only throw the ball with an underarm action.
- Players may run with the ball.
- If a player is tagged while in possession of the ball, he must return to the point of the tag before throwing the ball. For disputes over whether a tag was made, return the ball to where the previous player had it.
- Players cannot use a bounce pass.
- Points are awarded for catching the ball in the goal-receiving zone.
- A goal pass can only be made from the attacking quarter.

- Turnovers occur when the ball is dropped, intercepted, thrown out or thrown beyond the goal receiver's zone. All restarts from turnovers take place at the point of infringement.
- Following a tag, all players must stay two steps away from the person attempting to throw or pass the ball.
- After a tag the ball may be held without making a pass for about 5 seconds.
- Only the goal receiver is allowed in the goal receiver's zone.
- After a goal the person who passed the ball to the goal receiver becomes the goal receiver. The goal receiver joins the game as a field player.

▶ Variations

Pass Back

Pass Back rules (figure *c*):

- If a player is tagged with the ball outside of the attacking quarter, his first pass must be lateral or back towards his defensive goal.
- If a player passes forward after being tagged in possession outside of the attacking quarter, a turnover is declared.
- If a player is tagged in the attacking quarter, the ball may still be passed forward.

There are objectives behind the employment of the Pass Back rules. One is to teach on-ball attacking support play. If at least one player does not support from behind the on-ball attacker and that attacker is tagged while in possession of the ball, then a forward attacker has to run back to receive the next pass. This slows down the attack, and such receivers are easily seen and marked. Having a support player already in position allows a tagged player to quickly make the back pass. Another outcome is to teach that making a lateral pass is not necessarily a defensive tactic but an attacking one as it can change the point of attack. Yet a further objective of using the Pass Back rules variation is to encourage the player with the ball to pass before he is tagged. Passing before he is tagged maintains attacking momentum and discourages running with the ball when a pass is on.

The Pass Back rule variation in this game also provides an opportunity for the teacher or coach to address the concept of offensive depth. Having to pass the ball laterally or back towards one's defensive end encourages support play behind the on-ball player and allows players to see that though she has passed the ball back from her opponent's goal, she is still attacking. The only difference in her attacking play is that these attacks are being launched from a deeper defensive position than players normally associate with the concept of attacking in games. To defend against this type of attack requires the opposition to spread out over more of the court. This creates more space for the attacking team. Establishing this longitudinal space in a game is called offensive depth.

Continuing to allow the forward pass in the attacking quarter is also an important lesson for players because you do not want to teach a holding or defensive ploy in an area of the game (i.e., in front of the opponents' goal) in which players should be encouraged to take risks.

▶ Sport Language

- Leading
- Dodging
- V-leading
- Body language
- Double-teaming
- Lateral pass
- Back and around pass
- Support play

▶ Movement Skills

Players may need additional instruction in the following:

- Fundamentals of the underarm throw
- Catching a small ball with a Velcro glove
- Body language that indicates intended direction
- Man-to-man marking
- Leading into space to receive a pass
- Dodging

▶ Tactics and Strategies

The main tactical advantage in this game derives from the ability to lead into a space to receive a pass. For this movement to be successful, players should be taught how to lead, especially V-leads. Emphasis should be on quick dodging movements. Using width and depth when their team has the ball is extremely important. In the Pass Back game variation to Piltz Pass, it is also important to try to pass before being tagged.

Players also need to be taught to support the ball carrier. Teams should be encouraged to provide forward, lateral and back passes so the point of attack can be changed when confronted by the defence, thus allowing the attacking team to maintain its attacking momentum.

In defence, the main purpose is to congest the attacking zone. A second tactic is to try to slow down the opposition's counter-attack by tagging running players outside of their attacking quarter. Because they cannot score from this area, it allows the defence time to get organised to mark the attacking team's receiving players.

In the Pass Back variation that requires a player in possession of the ball outside of the attacking quarter to pass backwards on being tagged, players can be introduced to concepts such as zone defence and pressing. If the tagged player has an easy back pass available, the defensive player is better off dropping off the tagged player in the manner of a zone defence. However, if another player is required to come back in for support, that is the time to push forward (i.e., press) against the opposition.

A further way to teach tactics in this game is to make it a requirement for teams to develop offensive and defensive formations and play them for a time and then evaluate and modify them if they feel that is necessary. I have often found that students other than the technically advanced make valuable contributions when I adopt this approach to instruction.

▶ Attacking Skills

- Throwing and passing accurately and especially judging the correct amount of force or weight to apply to the ball
- Using body language to indicate where and when they want the ball
- Running and dodging
- Running and throwing
- Leading
- Finding space

▶ Defending Skills

- Recognising opponents' likely attacking options
- Marking players
- Reading and anticipating likely passes

- Intercepting passes
- Disrupting receivers' passes

▶ Questions

Attackers

Q: What are some basic movements attackers can make to provide passing options for their team?

A: Spread out so that they provide wide and deep passing options.

Q: Why is it important for at least one player on the same team to remain behind the person with the ball?

A: It provides an easy passing option if the forward receivers are marked.

A: In the Pass Back variation, if the person with the ball is tagged outside of the attacking quarter, they have to pass the ball backwards. Having a player there ensures that this pass can happen quickly.

Q: Why are short dodging movements, coupled with appropriate body language, important attacking skills?

A: The sudden, unexpected dodge provides the short time away from the marker to receive a pass. Long, steady movements are easily anticipated and therefore marked. The body language reveals to the passer the actual intended movement direction.

Defenders

Q: The attacking team loses possession of the ball in their attacking quarter. They are now the defending team. What should at least one of this team that is now defending attempt to do?

A: Try to tag the opposition player with the ball to slow down their counter-attack.

A: If the Pass Back variation is being played, it forces the team now attacking to make a back pass from this tag, stopping a quick break from a defensive to an attacking position and allows the defensive team to retreat and get organised to defend the attack.

Q: After tagging a player, should the tagger continue to mark the tagged player or move off to mark someone else?

A: It depends. In the attacking quarter the defender should mark the player to put pressure on the accuracy of her potential pass to her goal receiver. Outside of this area, the defender should perhaps leave her and try to mark potential receivers and force a turnover from the 5-second pass rule.

2

Attack and Defence Tactics

Should we use a man-to-man or a zone defence in this game?

How well are we using the fast break?

Do we need to position our players differently to do this?

Is it worth the risk to try for that play?

Do we provide enough depth in our defence? Do we let them get into our half too easily?

These are some of the questions that the games in this chapter pose and that you should use when teaching players the fundamental tactics associated with attack and defence in team games.

In this chapter I have not repeated the fact that players may need additional time to learn or master the movement skills that accompany these games. Many of these fundamental movements were covered in chapter 1, but that is not to say that the players will not need additional practice in those techniques. However, the difference between this chapter and chapter 1 needs to be emphasised. In chapter 1 the emphasis was on fundamental movement skills through the motivating medium of tactical games. In this chapter the emphasis is on teaching attacking and defensive tactics in team invasion games through the use of a limited number of fundamental movement skills.

Man-to-Man Defence

Man-to-man defence, or marking (also known as one-on-one defence), is a defensive strategy in which each player is assigned to defend and follow the movements of a single player on offense. This strategy is frequently employed in sports such as basketball, football and field hockey, although it is most obviously used in netball. In netball each player is assigned to a counterpart (e.g., centre guarding centre, goalkeeper guarding goal shooter). In games with less rigid court positions and movement restrictions (e.g., basketball), a player may be assigned to guard an opponent in a different position than his own. In these games and sports, the man-to-man strategy is not as rigid as it is in netball, and a player might switch the person he is marking if needed, or leave his marker for a moment to double-team an offensive player.

The advantage of the man-to-man defence is that everyone is sure of his defensive role. It also allows a team's best defender to stay on a player who has to be guarded at all times. The disadvantage is that it allows the offensive team to run screens more effectively, and it leaves weaker or slower defenders more exposed in classical mismatch opportunities. Although man-to-man marking might not necessarily be a good defensive system for very young players to employ in team games, understanding it is an important component of any player's education in game strategies.

This section provides a very simple introduction to man-to-man tactics, screening, mismatches, and the requirement for good communication in defence and for the offensive team to have considered set plays when playing against a man-to-man defence. The section also ensures further rehearsal of the fundamental movements employed in man-to-man defence and those required to play successfully against this game strategy.

Piggy in the Middle 1, 2 and 3

This traditional two-on-one game can, with modifications in instruction, be a great introduction to thinking about the rules and tactics associated with games and especially the strategy of man-to-man marking.

▸ Learning Objectives

Players will do the following:

- Be aware of game rules
- Mark players and not space
- Dodge to catch a ball
- Pass a ball

▸ Equipment

One ball (netball or similar) for every team of three players

▸ Formation

The team of three players (two passers and a marker) are confined to an area approximately 7 by 7 meters (about 8 by 8 yd). The player deemed the marker is also known as the piggy in the middle and always opposes the other two players. Three variations of this basic game are used to achieve the objectives.

▸ Recipe

Piggy in the Middle 1

In the first game, all players are confined to the square. The two passers pass the ball back and forth trying to avoid having it intercepted by the marker (figure a). The passers cannot run with the ball. One basic rule that is important for the outcomes of these games is that the marker (the pig) cannot snatch the ball from a passer. Have players play the game for about 30 seconds and then rotate positions. If the marker (the pig in the middle) intercepts the ball before the 30 seconds of play are up, the tradition of the game is that he becomes a passer, and the person whose pass he intercepted becomes the 'pig in the middle.' Discuss how successful the passers were in passing the ball back and forth.

Piggy in the Middle 2

In the second game, with all players confined to the square, instruct the players to do their best to not allow the pig to intercept the ball for 30 seconds. Although the game in practice is exactly the same as the first game, the instruction of 'do not allow the pig to intercept the ball for 30 seconds' tends to have the effect of how the passers pass the ball. Have the players play the game and then rotate positions (figure b). Observe any change in tactics employed by the passers.

Piggy in the Middle 3

In the third game, with all players again confined to the square, instruct the players to try to make as many passes as possible in the 30 seconds of game time (figure c). If the marker 'pig in the middle' intercepts a pass, it results in a deduction of one pass from the passers' score, but the ball is returned to the passers, who continue to try to make as many passes as possible in their allotted time. Rotate the positions so everyone has two turns at passing and one as the pig in the middle. A passer's score is the total number of passes he accumulated in his two turns as a passer. Observe any change in tactics employed by the passers or the piggy in the middle.

▸ Rules

- Passers may pass the ball using chest or bounce passes.
- Passers can dodge to receive a pass.
- Passers cannot run with the ball.
- The defender (the piggy in the middle) must maintain a distance of at least one step from a passer or receiver.
- The defender cannot snatch the ball from a passer.

▸ Variations

Variations for this game could include changing the type of ball used and the types of passes allowed (e.g., no bounce passes).

▸ Sport Language

- Attacker
- Defender
- Man-to-man marking

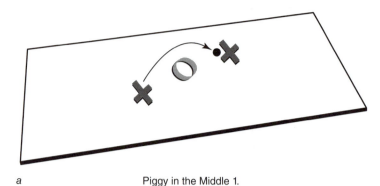

a　　　　　　Piggy in the Middle 1.

b　　　　　　Piggy in the Middle 2.

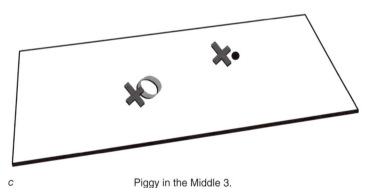

c　　　　　　Piggy in the Middle 3.

▶ Tactics and Strategies

The variations in this game, which is usually only played by quite young children, introduce students to the idea of thinking about rules and marking. In the first variation the very name of the game, Piggy in the Middle, encourages the pig to play in the middle of the space between the passers. The 'pig' tends to intercept passes when the ball is passed short or lobbed in a manner that allows him time to get in position to catch the ball. In the second variation you

will probably see most students playing as they did in the first game, though perhaps a little more cautiously. However, if they think about the rule that the pig (defender) cannot snatch the ball from a passer, then they may realise that the easiest way to keep the ball for 30 seconds is not to pass it!

In the third game they must pass the ball to score points, so just keeping the ball is not an option. However, most pigs (defenders) in the middle will maintain a middle position between the passers when they should man-to-man mark the receiver. This simple game provides an introduction to man-to-man marking.

There is a fair play issue to consider with this game. Is Piggy in the Middle 2, in which the passers can achieve the game outcome by not passing the ball, in the spirit of the game (i.e., is it fair play)? Should not a game give both teams a chance of success? Has the game fallen over, and do we need to add rules to make it fair?

▶ Attacking Skills

- Disguising the direction of passes
- Dodging for a pass
- Using body language to indicate where the ball should be thrown

▶ Defending Skills

- Thinking about the rules of the game and how best use them to one's advantage
- Anticipating likely passes
- Positioning oneself close to the receiver one is marking

▶ Questions

General

Q: What is man-to-man marking?

A: It is when one player defends against one other player. Typically, he matches up against that player for most of the game (e.g., the defensive left half in field hockey marks the attacking right wing). Sometimes defenders change the player they mark, but at all times the objective is to have one player on the team marking one player on the opponents' team.

Q: Marking and receiving passes in this game require what type of movements?

A: Quick dodging movements.

Piggy in the Middle 2

Q: What is the objective of the game?

A: To keep the ball for 30 seconds.

Q: What are the rules relating to defending against the passers?

A: Defenders cannot stand closer than one step away from the passer and cannot snatch the ball from a passer.

Q: What is the easiest way of achieving the game objective within the rules of the game?

A: One passer just stands still holding on to the ball because the rules prevent the defender from snatching the ball.

Piggy in the Middle 3

Q: What is the objective for the passers?

A: To make as many passes as possible in 30 seconds.

Q: What is the name of the type of marking best suited for Piggy in the Middle 3?

A: Man-to-man marking.

Q: In this variation, whom should the piggy in the middle mark, or defend?

A: The person without the ball.

Q: How closely should the piggy mark him?

A: As close as possible—probably beside him.

Q: What must a receiver do to receive a pass when being marked that closely?

A: Use body language or call for passes and dodge to receive the ball. He should not stand still!

Hoop Pass

While Piggy in the Middle hinted at man-to-man marking, this game absolutely emphasises it. With the players much closer to each other and with the defender starting the game with the call 'Play', it closely resembles restarts in netball. To play well, passer and receiver have to coordinate their moves by making extensive use of body language, especially eye contact.

▶ Learning Objectives

Players will do the following:

- Man-to-man mark
- Triangle mark
- Dodge to receive a pass
- Feint movements
- Catch a ball while moving
- Pass to space

▶ Equipment

- One ball (netball or similar) for every three players
- One hoop for every three players

▶ Formation

Three players are confined to an area approximately 7 by 7 metres, or about 8 by 8 yards. One player, the passer, occupies the hoop that is placed in the middle of the square. Another player is the receiver, and the third player is the marker.

▶ Recipe

The passer in the hoop starts with the ball and tries to pass to the receiver. All players start from a stationary position. To start the game, the defender (marker) calls 'Play'. The passer and the receiver try to make a successful pass. The attackers (passer and receiver) have 10 attempts to make successful passes for a score out of 10. The receiver uses dodges and feints to get into space to receive the ball from the passer in the hoop (see figure *a*). The defender tries to intercept, spoil or prevent a pass (see figure *b*). After a successful or unsuccessful pass, the ball is always returned to the passer. The defender restarts the game when they are ready by calling 'Play'.

Each successful pass is worth 1 point for the passer and the receiver. After the 10 passing attempts have been completed, the score is noted and the players rotate positions. Because both the passer and the receiver are allocated points for each successful pass, the passing player should try to give good, catchable passes to reinforce the old adage 'it takes two to make a pass'.

The scoring system is shown in table 2.1.

▶ Rules

- The receiver and defender must maintain a distance of at least two steps from the hoop and passer (see figure *c*). This is to stop the receiver from standing right beside the passer and being given the ball.

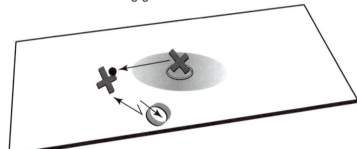

a   The attacker makes a lead to create space and receives a pass.

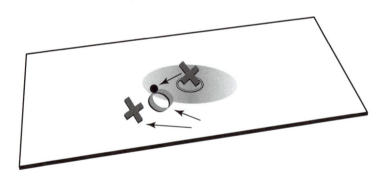

b   The defender intercepts the ball and play is restarted.

c   The attacker receives a pass in the restricted area. Play restarts.

Table 2.1 Scoring Systems for Hoop Pass

Round	1 + 2v3	1 + 3v2	2 + 3v1	Totals
Player 1	6	5		11
Player 2	6		7	13
Player 3		5	7	12

• No deliberate body contact is allowed.

› Variation

This game can be played by experienced players using specific sports equipment (e.g., football or field hockey).

› Sport Language

• Emptying the space
• Triangle marking
• Feinting
• Anticipating
• Man-to-man marking

› Tactics and Strategies

To receive passes, the receiver needs to employ quick changes of movement. For example, a quick feint to her right to trick the defender out of the intended receiving space (empty the space) followed by a dodge back left to receive the ball. These types of movements, along with interposing her body to block the defender so she can receive the pass wide on the side furthest from the passer, are the most obvious tactics for the receiver.

The defender needs to try to triangle mark the receiver. This is achieved by marking to the side and slightly in front of the receiver. In this way, she tries to dictate the direction of the pass. It also allows her a chance to intercept passes while also covering a lobbed pass.

› Attacking Skills

• Dodging
• Emptying the space
• Blocking
• Using body language
• Faking movements
• Giving lob passes

› Defending Skills

• Use man-to-man marking
• Using triangle marking tactics
• Anticipating the timing of passes
• Observing the opponent's body language for clues to possible movements

› Questions

Attackers

Q: What type of movement is most successful in this type of game?

A: Quick dodges to or away from the passer.

Q: What can attackers do to coordinate their movements with the timing of the pass?

A: Use body language, hand or eye movements, or call as they move. They should practise these moves.

Q: How can an attacker escape from a man-to-man marker by using the stationary passer?

A: She can run the marker towards the passer so the marker cannot stay beside the attacker unless she barges into the passer (this is an early introduction to the concept of a screen).

Defenders

Q: What are the best marking options to prevent successful passes?

A: Man-to-man marking to the side and slightly in front of the receiver, known as triangle marking.

Q: Do defenders have a better chance of intercepting long or short passes?

A: Defenders have a better chance of intercepting long passes (the ball is in the air longer), so they should try to encourage those types of passes by the way they position themselves.

Q: What are the advantages and disadvantages of marking in front, behind or beside the receiver?

A: In front: It is difficult to see the opponent but forces a lob and more easily intercepted passes.

Beside: It is easy for the passer to pass to receivers on the side further from the defender.

Behind: The marker can anticipate passes but will have difficulty preventing or spoiling them.

Q: Is there a defensive advantage to keeping some space between oneself and the receiver?

A: Yes. Doing so sometimes stops the defender from responding to a fake move so quickly, or from receiving little knocks, which can put her off balance. It also forces more distance between the passer and the receiver.

Challenge

Learning about the strategy of man-to-man marking continues in this game. However, an additional concept associated with that strategy is introduced—namely, an even match-up of players or an uneven match-up (mismatch). This refers to having players as equal in skill as possible marking each other or having mismatches between the players to engineer an advantage for the team (e.g., when being tall is an advantage, moving your players around the playing area so that at a key moment your tallest player is marked by their shortest one).

▶ Learning Objectives

Players will do the following:

- Understand the concepts of match-ups and mismatches
- Use man-to-man marking
- Dodge
- Receive a ball
- Pass a ball
- Block players' intended direction of movement

▶ Equipment

- One ball (netball or similar) per six players
- Two hoops
- Pens and paper

▶ Formation

Two opposing teams have three players each. Three attacking players of one team are in an area approximately 7 by 7 metres, or about 8 by 8 yards. Two of these attackers stand in the hoops that are placed near each other near the middle of the square (see figure *a*). The attackers in the hoops must stay in the hoops. A third attacking player (the receiver) receives passes from the hoop players and may move anywhere in the square except for the space between the two hoops. It is best to think of the space between the hoops as a wall. One opposing player, who will try to defend the passes to the receiver, also stands in the square and has the same movement restrictions as the attacking receiver.

▶ Recipe

Two opposing teams of three are chosen. Each team has to announce the order in which its players will be the receivers. Teams should write this down and hand the playing order to the opposition. Once this is done, teams can then decide the order in which they will play against the attackers (i.e., who will mark the opposition players).

The passers in the hoop start with the ball. The defender, when ready, calls 'Play', and the game starts. The passers try to make as many passes to their receiver as possible while the defender does his best to intercept, prevent or spoil those passes. This game is continuous. Successful or unsuccessful passes are immediately returned to the hoop players (return passes are not contested by the opponent), and the game continues for an agreed time (e.g., 20 seconds). Each successful pass is worth 1 point to the passing, or attacking, team (see figure *b*). After the agreed time has elapsed, the score is noted and the teams change positions.

▶ Rules

- Both the receiver and the defender must maintain a distance of two steps from the hoops. This is to stop the attackers from standing beside each other and handing off the ball.
- Hoop players can pass to each other (introducing the concept of keeping possession of the ball), but these passes do not count as points (see figure *c*).
- The defender cannot snatch the ball from a hoop player.
- No deliberate body contact is allowed.
- Teams must play their receivers in the order announced before the start of the game.
- Teams play alternatively (i.e., team A occupies the hoops and tries to make passes; then team B occupies the hoops; then back to team A until everyone has had a turn as a receiver).

▶ Variation

You may wish to restrict the height of passes (e.g., below head height).

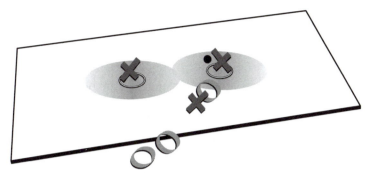

a   The attacking team have announced their playing order. The first defender steps in while their teammates wait on the sideline.

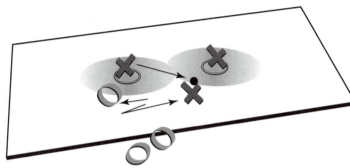

b   The receiver has caught a pass outside the restricted area and scored a point.

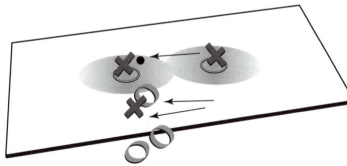

c   If passes to the receiver are unavailable, the attackers in the hoops can pass between themselves. These passes are not worth any points.

▶ Sport Language

- Match-ups
- Mismatches

▶ Tactics and Strategies

Because each team must announce its receiving player order before the game starts, the opposition team can discuss who will attempt to mark the opposition's players. The strategy for consideration is whether to choose even match-ups or mismatches against the opposition.

▶ Attacking Skills

- Using body language
- Dodging
- Quick interpassing
- Emptying the space
- Doubling around players
- One-two passing

▶ Defending Skills

- Anticipating
- Triangle marking
- Using peripheral vision

▶ Questions

Defenders

Q: Once they know the opposition's playing order, what do teams need to decide as part of their strategy for winning the game?

A: Whether to use even match-ups or mismatches.

Even match-ups: Playing one's fastest player against the opposition's fastest player.

Mismatch: Playing one's fastest player against the opposition's slowest player.

Q: How can defenders exploit a height advantage?

A: They can mark slightly in front when defending, forcing longer, slower passes that they will have more time to intercept.

Q: How might teams use a mismatch?

A: They might sacrifice their not-so-fast player against the opposition's fastest player, but put their fastest player against the opposition's slowest. The hope is that their not-so-fast player will play extraordinarily well and that their fastest player will completely shut out the opposition's slowest player from scoring.

Attackers

Q: What types of passes are best for the slowest player to receive?

A: Short passes that have less time for interception and require short, quick dodges to receive so that the speed difference between the players is not so important.

Q: How can teams (attackers) use a speed advantage to help you score?

A: Longer passes, which require the defender to move further to try to prevent the passes.

Round the Outside

A variation of man-to-man marking is double-teaming. Instead of using one player against one other player, a team uses double-teaming to place two defenders onto one attacker—they double-team him! This is usually employed when a team perceives that one player in the opposition is so good that he requires two people to mark him. It can also be a good tactic to use when a team realises that one of its defenders has delayed one of the attackers or put him in a position in which a second member of the team could give immediate assistance and most likely secure a turnover of possession. Of course, the downside of the tactic is that the player who is double-teamed can either elude both defenders or pass the ball, leaving a mismatch of attackers against defenders.

This game also introduces the concept of maintaining possession. Because it is harder to pass to someone marked by two players than one, keeping possession and passing only when the pass is on (i.e., the pass is most likely to be completed and not intercepted), is a required tactic.

Learning Objectives

Players will do the following:

- Learn the concepts associated with double-teaming
- Maintain possession
- Dodge
- Receive and release the ball quickly
- Mark
- Understand the need to talk on defence

Equipment

- One ball (netball or similar)
- Bibs for distinguishing teams

Formation

Create two teams of five players. The attacking team places one player along each side of a defined area (e.g., 10 by 10 m, or about 11 by 11 yd). One player (the main receiver) stands in the square. Two opposition players from the defending team also go into the square to mark the main receiver and try to restrict the passing options of the attacking team. One of the other three defenders becomes the timekeeper, announcing when the playing time is up. The other two defenders call out the score, which is the number of passes the opposition's receiver inside the square receives.

Recipe

The attacking team has 30 seconds to score as many goals as possible. Goals are achieved when the main receiving player inside the square receives a pass from a team-mate on the outside of the square. A successful pass to the receiver, inside the square, is a goal and is worth 1 point (see figure a). The four passing players on the outside of the square can also pass to each other to maintain possession and better position the ball for a pass to the receiver (see figure b). However, these passes do not earn points. Passes must be below head height. The passers on the outside can move up and down their side of the square, but they cannot move when they have the ball. The main receiver and markers can move anywhere in the square.

The two markers (defenders) in the square try to spoil, intercept or delay the attacking team's attempts to pass around the outside and to the main receiver inside the square (see figure c). The defenders cannot snatch the ball from a passer or receiver. Following successful and unsuccessful plays or turnovers, the ball is passed back to a passer on the outside of the square and play continues. The passes back to the attackers outside of the square are free passes.

Teams and players rotate after 30 seconds and a short break. Receivers and defenders need to discuss their tactics before each time starts. The game can last until each of the five players has had a turn as the main receiver. The total scores of each game are the team's score.

A timekeeper is required. The attacking team can count its score aloud, or each game can have a scorer.

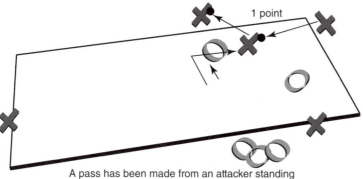

1 point

a A pass has been made from an attacker standing on the side of the area to the receiver in the playing area. The receiver passes back to an outside player.

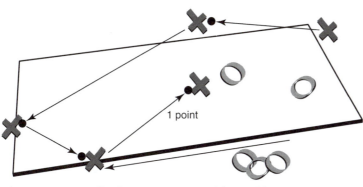

1 point

b Attackers can pass around the outside.

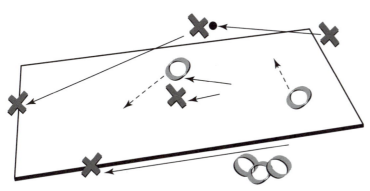

c The defenders have successfully stopped passes being made to the centre player.

▶ Rules

Attackers

- Attackers may pass the ball around or across the outsides of the square.
- Attackers can move up or down their side of the square when they are not in possession of the ball.

- Attackers cannot move when they have the ball.
- Passes must be below head height.

Defenders

- The two defenders may move anywhere inside the square.
- The defenders may double-team the receiver, but they must not physically hold on to the receiver to restrain movements.

Attackers and Defenders

If passes into the square to the receiver are completed (caught) or intercepted, the ball must be returned to the attackers on the outside of the square without interference from the defenders, as each team only has a set time to score points, and it is unfair to delay the return of the balls to the attackers.

▶ Variation

This game can be played by experienced players using specific sports equipment (e.g., football or field hockey).

▶ Sport Language

- Channeling
- Peripheral vision
- Maintaining possession
- Body language

▶ Tactics and Strategies

The players outside of the square need to pass around the outside (or across the square) to keep providing various passing options to their receiver inside the square. They have to stay aware of when a pass into the square (a goal) is possible. Passers on the outside also need to be patient and not needlessly throw a goal pass that isn't likely to be successful.

The defenders, or markers, need to communicate and try to restrict the number of goal passes because of their point value, but they also have to try to prevent the easier, across side passes. Defenders also have to make decisions about man-to-man marking, what passes they will allow and how they will put pressure on receivers or passers.

The game requires good communication among all players. The game also forces the defenders to think about not just preventing a pass but how to make the play as slow as possible.

▶ Attacking Skills

- Emptying the space
- Dodging for passes
- Using body language
- Disguising passes
- Patience

▶ Defending Skills

- Double-teaming
- Forcing, or channeling, passes in one direction
- Deciding which passes to allow
- Anticipating
- Using peripheral vision
- Discussing tactics

▶ Questions

General

Q: What is a fake?

A: When a player pretends to do something while always intending to do something else—for example, start to move to the right and then suddenly go to the left, which was always the way the player intended to go.

Attackers

Q: How can the players around the outside of the square without the ball support the player with the ball to make successful passes?

A: By moving towards him along the sides of the square, thus providing a pass that is difficult to intercept. They can also call and direct passes to a team-mate who is available to receive a pass.

Q: What sort of movements should the receiver make to evade the two defenders?

A: Fast, dodging-type movements.

Q: What types of body language can the receiver use to communicate with his players on the outside of the square?

A: The receiver can use hand movements to indicate the direction in which he is going to move. Eye contact and facial expressions can also indicate if and where he is ready to receive a pass.

Defenders

Q: Is it more important to mark the receiver inside the square or to try to prevent passes around the outside?

A: It is more important to mark the receiver because a pass to him is the only way the attackers can score points.

Q: What is the defenders' easiest form of communication to each other, and why is it so important?

A: Talking, because although the defenders cannot always see each other, they still need to know what each other are doing in order to work as a team.

Q: Can defenders put pressure on the passes around the outside?

A: Yes, defenders can force the attackers to pass one way. They cannot stop all of the attacker's passing options, though, because that will leave easy point-value passes to the receiver inside the square.

Zone Defence

I have found a castle analogy useful in describing zone defence to young players. I ask them to think of their goal as their castle and explain that, on defence, they have to protect their castle. They do this by occupying assigned zones around the castle. They guard that area by marking any player that tries to come into it. They do this whether or not that person is in possession of the ball or scoring object.

I further explain that if the person coming into their zone is in possession of the ball, they should think of themselves as the on-ball defender. If the ball is being brought in from the other side but opposition players are still advancing into their zone, they should think of themselves as the off-ball support defender. Another way to explain the off-ball defender is to call her the help-side defender.

The simplest zone defence system involves players placing themselves evenly around the perimeter of the defensive area. Against an attack, on-ball defenders confront the opposition by advancing slightly towards them while the off-ball defenders provide cover defence. If the attack swings across the front of the goal to attack from the other side, the defence slides across with the attack (a sliding zone defence), and the defenders change roles (i.e., the cover defence becomes the on-ball defenders and the previous on-ball defenders become the off-ball defenders). In all cases, players maintain their relative positions to each other.

Although simple in concept, zone defence is still a very effective defensive strategy in all invasion games that require players to defend a central goal. Its weakness is that one defensive player may be required to mark two offensive players, or a defensive player may lose her discipline and come out of the defence, leaving space for the opposition to attack. Employing zone defence successfully requires player discipline and cooperation.

The games used to teach zone defence in this section are extremely simple. The beauty of the games in this section is that, to play them successfully, teams have to employ zone defences.

It is important to play the following three games in sequence. Once players have learned the basic game Zone Defence, the two games that follow, Outlet and Fast Break, progressively introduce more sophisticated attacking and defending concepts.

Zone Defence

The beauty of this game is the way the teaching moment so readily occurs and allows you to pause the game and ask questions that lead to a basic explanation of zone defence. This occurs because two defenders naturally defend the two cones, leaving the third defender without a specific defensive task. This player often instinctively sets up in front of and between the other two defenders. This establishes a triangular defensive pattern with one of the defenders 'pointing' the zone defence.

▶ Learning Objectives

Players will do the following:

- Learn the concepts associated with zone defence
- Adjust their playing positions in relation to the direction of the attack
- Point on defence
- Throw a ball accurately at the cones
- Use time-outs

▶ Equipment

- Four hoops
- Four cones
- One ball (netball or similar)
- Bibs to distinguish the teams

▶ Formation

Create two teams of five, with three players from each team on the court (a third of a netball or a volleyball court). Place two large cones inside two hoops at each end of the court area. The distance between the cones is not set, but ensure that the width between them is such that one player cannot mark both cones at the same time. Play can be in front of and behind the cones (see figure a).

▶ Recipe

Players move up the court by passing the ball (they can take a step with the ball but they cannot run with it) and then attempt to score a goal by throwing the ball at the cones. A goal is scored if a cone is struck or knocked over. Defensive players attempt to block or intercept passes and throws at the cones, but they must stay at least one step away from the player with the ball. Opposition players are not allowed to take, or snatch, the ball from someone holding it. Defensive players cannot stand inside the hoops where the cones are or hold on to the cones to stop them from being knocked over. Play is continuous unless the ball goes out or a goal is scored. Players use a pass-off by the defending team's goal cones to restart the game.

Have the players play 3v3 for approximately 5 to 7 minutes. Allow the substitutes of each team to call two time-outs of 30 seconds to 1 minute in each period of play. They should use this time to substitute players and talk tactics.

▶ Rules

Attackers

- Attackers may pass the ball in any manner including bounce passes.
- Attackers may take a step and pivot with the ball.
- Running or walking with the ball is not permitted.
- Attackers may play or position themselves anywhere in front of, to the side of or behind the cones.

Defenders

- Defenders must always be at least one step away from any attackers.
- Defenders may block shots at cones with any part of the body, including the legs, but they must not strike the ball with their feet in a kicking motion.
- All interceptions result in an automatic turnover of possession.
- Defenders may not stand inside the hoops.
- Defenders may not hold on to or secure in any way the cones that constitute the goals in this game.

General

- The ball hitting or knocking over a cone is a goal.
- After a goal the ball is turned over to the defenders, who become the attackers.
- Each team is allowed to call two time-outs in the time period set for the game to make substitutions or discuss tactics.

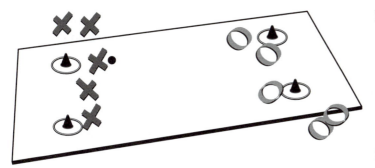

a Basic formation.

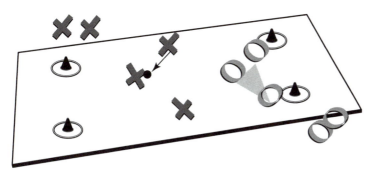

b Players form a zone defence as part of the game.

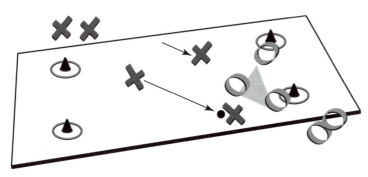

c The zone slides as the ball is passed across the front of the goals.

▶ Variation

With advanced players in specific sports, the single cones could be replaced with mini-goals while maintaining the same formation. For example, in football, two small goals that attackers would try to pass the ball through for a goal would result in the same defensive formation.

▶ Sport Language

- Zone defence
- Pointing on defence
- Sliding defence
- Time-outs
- Player rotation

▶ Tactics and Strategies

Having two cones for players to defend forces a pyramid defence with one player in front of each cone and another out in front of them. The consequence of this is that a zone defence is established (see figure *b*). The player in front of the cones points the defence. It is important that the person pointing the defence moves across the front of the cones if the attackers shift the point of their attack (see figure *c*). If the attackers pass the ball behind the goals, the defenders need to communicate and quickly adjust their positions to maintain the shape of their defensive pattern. Encourage a discussion of a moving defence, teamwork and defending and attacking together.

The attackers need to learn to move quickly off the ball, and when they have the ball, to learn to pass to the space where they anticipate their players are moving to. Holding on to the ball for too long gives the defenders time to organise their defence of the cones. If the defenders are all in position, the attackers need to be patient and pass the ball around quickly to look for an opening to shoot at the cones or encourage the defenders to try for an interception and expose their goal.

The placement of the cones can make the game favour the defenders or the attackers. The closer the cones are to each other, the easier it is for the defenders; the further they are apart, the easier it is for the attackers.

If students don't naturally pick up the zone concept, stop the game at an appropriate teaching moment and ask them the questions at the end of this game description.

▶ Attacking Skills

- Maintaining possession
- Disguising intention to shoot
- Accurate throws

▶ Defending Skills

- Pyramid zone defence
- Sliding defence
- Intercepting passes

▶ Questions

Attackers

Q: Why is it important to pass quickly to team-mates?

A: Quick passes force the defenders to keep adjusting their positions while retreating. This can lead to confusion in the defence and easy chances for the attackers to throw the ball at the cones.

Q: If the defenders are well set up in defence, what are the best attacking options?

A: Attackers should position themselves so they can pass both across and behind the defenders to force them to constantly adjust their defensive positions.

Q: Against a set defence, what type of shots might give attackers the best chance of scoring goals?

A: Feinting the first or even second throw. Passers should try to get the defender to commit to a block before actually releasing the ball.

Defenders

Q: When there is a turnover, what is an the option for the defending team?

A: The defending team can counter-attack. This requires the players without the ball to quickly find space in which to receive a pass.

Q: How many players should directly defend the cones?

A: Two.

Q: Where should the third defending player stand?

A: Out in front to point the defence and create a pyramid defensive pattern.

Q: Are there any advantages for the defenders in standing slightly out in front of the cones?

A: Yes. Doing so forces the attackers to play further away from the goal resulting in longer and more difficult shots.

Q: If the attackers pass the ball around (e.g., from left to right) and attack from the other side, how should the defenders move to stop their attack?

A: They should slide from left to right with the attack.

Q: Is talking in defence important? Why?

A: Yes, because in many games defenders cannot see all of the attackers, and they need advice on where to move to ensure that all attackers are being marked.

Q: Who in the defence has the best view of the attacking team's options?

A: Usually the defensive player furthest back from the attack. In this game that is usually the player on the side opposite the point of attack.

Outlet

In the same way that employing a zone defence is basic to invasion games that require the defence of a central goal, so too is the next play or pass often employed when the defenders secure or intercept the ball from the attackers out in front of their goal. When possible, the first pass following the interception should be out from in front of their goal towards the sideline. This type of pass is generally known as an outlet pass.

This game differs only slightly from Zone Defence. The rules of the game force the teams to use an outlet pass.

▶ Learning Objectives

Players will do the following:

- Learn the tactical concept of an outlet pass
- Learn the pass and follow movement associated with the outlet pass
- Throw, catch and disguise passes
- Understand the importance of quick transitions from attack to defence

▶ Equipment

- Eight hoops
- Four large cones
- One ball (netball or similar)
- Bibs to distinguish the teams

▶ Formation

Two teams of five have three players each on the court (a rectangular area such as a third of a netball or a volleyball court). Place two large cones inside two hoops in from each end of the court area as in the manner of the previous game, Zone Defence. Play can be in front of and behind the cones. Place an additional four hoops, two on each side, outside of the court near the halfway point. The two players not on the court from both teams (the outlet players) stand in these hoops, one on each side of the court nearer their defensive end (see figure a).

▶ Recipe

Players move up the court by passing the ball (they can take a step with the ball but they cannot run with it) and then attempt to knock over or hit one of the cones by throwing the ball at it to score a goal. Defensive players attempt to block or intercept passes (see figure b), but they must stay at least one step away from the player with the ball. Opposition players are not allowed to snatch the ball from someone holding it. Defensive players cannot stand inside the hoops where the cones are or hold on to them to stop them from being knocked over. Play is continuous unless the ball goes out or a goal is scored. Players use a pass-off by the defending team's goal to restart the game. However, such passes must be outlet passes.

All turnovers in a team's defensive half, including a scored goal, requires the ball to be passed to one of that team's outlet players standing in a hoop. The outlet player passes the ball back into play, changes places with the person who threw the ball, and the game continues (see figure c).

Have the players play for approximately 5 to 7 minutes allowing each team to call two time-outs of 30 seconds to 1 minute in each period of play. They should use this time to talk tactics.

Note: If a team loses the ball while on attack but regains it while still in the attacking half, that team does not make an outlet pass.

▶ Rules

Attackers

- Attackers may pass the ball in any manner including bounce passes.
- Attackers are allowed to take a step and pivot with the ball.
- Running or walking with the ball is not permitted.
- Attackers may position themselves anywhere in front of, to the side of or behind the cones.

Defenders

- Defenders must always remain one step away from the attackers.
- Defenders may block shots at cones with any part of the body, including the legs, but they must not strike the ball with their feet in a kicking motion.
- All interceptions result in an automatic turnover of possession. If the turnover of possession

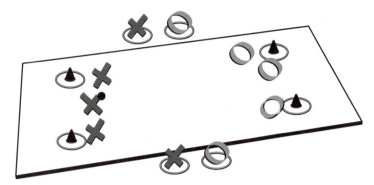

a   Basic formation. Note the outlet players standing in hoops.

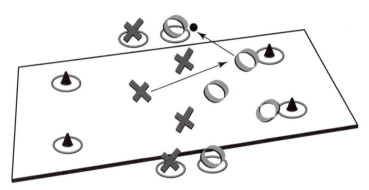

b   A defender intercepts a shot and then makes the outlet pass.

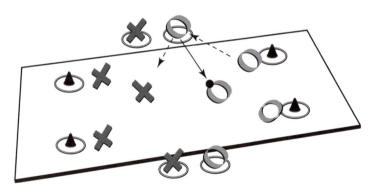

c   The outlet player passes the ball back into play and joins the game. The player is replaced in the outlet hoop by the player who intercepted.

occurs in the defender's defensive half, the next pass from the defender **must** be an outlet pass.

- Defenders may not stand inside the hoops.
- Defenders may not hold on to or secure in any way the cones that constitute the goals.

General

- The ball hitting or knocking over a cone is a goal.
- After a goal, the ball is turned over to the defenders, who become the attackers.
- Each team is allowed to call two time-outs in the time period set for the game to discuss tactics.
- Any turnover in a team's defensive half requires that team to make an outlet pass to one of the players standing in a hoop outside the court. This pass cannot be contested or intercepted by the opposition—it is a free pass. On receiving the pass, the outlet player passes the ball back into play to one of his team-mates and joins the game. The player who made the pass to the outlet player now stands in the hoop and becomes an outlet player. In this way each team maintains only three players on court.

▶ Variation

One variation to this game is to allow the pass back into play from the outlet player to be contested. This rule variation still ensures that the outlet pass is achieved, but it allows an attacking defence by encouraging the player most forward on the defensive team to slow down the counter-attack by putting pressure on the pass back into play. It also forces more complex decision making on the part of the passer and more off-the-ball movement by the receivers to get the ball.

The downside of the tactic of a defensive player defending the pass back into play is that it can leave a defender upfield, giving the new attacking team, if players move quickly, a three-on-two player advantage to attack their goals.

▶ Sport Language

- Outlet pass
- Attacking defence

▶ Tactics and Strategies

The main objective of this game is to teach players the tactical play of using outlet passes away from in front of their goal after they have secured possession of the ball from the attackers. This is an important tactical play in games such as football, field hockey and basketball, in which the goal is in the middle of the end line. If the defenders, who have just secured possession of the ball, make a mistake and give it back to the attackers, it is better that this occur near the sideline away from the danger area immediately in front of their goal.

Another important factor to consider for the use of this pass is that the ball is passed to an area where the opposition is least likely to have any of their previously attacking players. Thus, the pass has a better chance of being successfully completed. In addition, defenders are more inclined to allow this type of pass because it is less threatening to them in terms of their new priority, which is to now defend their own goal.

Another aspect of the outlet pass is to teach your players to follow their passes. This almost becomes a 'pass and double around action'. Take the time to explain this movement and how effective it is in games.

Finally, allowing the outlet pass as a free pass gives the team now defending time to retreat to defend against the next attack. Often in these games, some players neglect their defensive duties, and this playing scenario makes their lack of defensive commitment obvious. Such observations might become discussion topics in any time-outs called by the team.

▶ Attacking Skills

- Passing
- Maintaining possession
- Disguising intention to shoot

▶ Defending Skills

- Outlet passing
- Pyramid zone defence
- Attacking defence

▶ Questions

General Questions

Q: What is the name of the pass to the players in the hoop?

A: Outlet pass.

Q: What advantage does the attacking team gain if the defenders who have just secured a turnover of the ball pass it wide?

A: It gives them more time to get back and organise their defence.

Q: How do players decide when to take risks in a game?

A: The state of the game dictates risk taking. Attackers usually take more risks than defenders.

Attackers

Q: At a turnover, what is the responsibility of the player furthest back from the attack?

A: To drop back and prevent an easy shot at goal or to mark an opposition player who might have remained on attack.

Q: At a turnover, what is the responsibility of the player most forward on attack?

A: To try to slow down the opposition's counter-attack and force another turnover.

Defenders

Q: What are some of the tactical advantages for the defending team having just intercepted the ball in passing wide (i.e., using an outlet pass)?

A: It immediately takes the ball away from in front of the goal.

A: It starts to stretch the opposition's attack if they try to defend upfield.

A: The opposition is not likely to have any of its players in this part of the playing area and are likely to be less concerned with allowing attackers this pass.

A: Mistakes away from the goal are not as serious as mistakes in front of the goal.

Q: What might be the tactical disadvantage of passing directly out in front of the goal?

A: A turnover in front of the goal could give the opposition an easy shot at goal.

Q: When might defenders risk an outlet pass right in front of their goal?

A: When such a pass is on, when they are losing with time running out, or to change the pattern of how they are playing.

Fast Break

The two previous zone defence games focused on the zone defence pattern. The focus for this game changes from defence to counter-attack from a zone defence position. When a team drops back to set up a zone defence around its goal, it gives up to the opposition quite a lot of undisputed territory. This encourages the opposition to bring a large number of players forward into the attack. A quick-thinking defensive team, upon recovering possession of the ball, can exploit this characteristic of attacking against their zone defence by looking to mount quick counter-attacks. The type of counter-attack that is the focus of this game is known as a fast break.

▶ Learning Objectives

Players will do the following:

- Learn the concepts associated with the fast break
- Learn the importance of counter-attacking
- Lead on attack
- Make space for outlet passes
- Perform one-two passes

▶ Equipment

- Eight hoops
- Four cones
- One ball (netball or similar)
- Bibs to distinguish the teams

▶ Formation

Two teams of five have three players each on the court (a rectangular area such as a third of a netball or a volleyball court). Place two large cones inside two hoops in from each end of the court area in exactly the same manner of the previous two games, Zone Defence and Outlet. Play can be in front of or behind the cones. Place an additional four hoops, two on each side, outside of the court near the halfway point. The two players not on the court from both teams (the outlet players) stand in these hoops, one on each side of the court nearest their defensive end (see figure a).

▶ Recipe

Players move up the court by passing the ball (they can take a step with the ball but they cannot run with it) and then attempt to knock over or hit one of the cones by throwing the ball at it to score a goal. Defensive players attempt to block or intercept passes, but they must stay at least one step away from the player with the ball. Opposition players are not allowed to snatch the ball from someone holding it. Defensive players cannot stand inside the hoops where the cones are or hold on to them to stop them from being knocked over. Play is continuous unless the ball goes out or a goal is scored. Players use a pass-off by the defending team's goal to restart the game.

All turnovers in a team's defensive half, including after a goal has been scored, require the ball to be passed to one of that team's outlet players, who may, while still at this stage remaining outside of the playing area, move out of his hoop at halfway and come back to receive the ball (i.e., dodge back). The outlet player uses a one-two pass to pass the ball back into play to the player who just passed her the ball, and joins the game (see figure b).

The outlet player on the other side of the playing area also joins the game but does so forward of halfway (see figure b). Her role is to provide a further passing option forward to act like a fast break. The two players who did not pass the ball to the outlet player change places with the previous outlet players by going and standing in the hoops at the halfway point (see figure c). In this way, two players are always dropping out or into the game and everyone is kept involved.

Have players play for approximately 5 to 7 minutes. Allow the substitutes of each team to call two time-outs of 30 seconds to 1 minute in each period of play. They should use this time to substitute players and talk tactics.

Opposition players waiting in hoops cannot contest passes from the opposition team. *Note:* If a team loses the ball while on attack but regains it while still in the attacking half, it does not make an outlet pass.

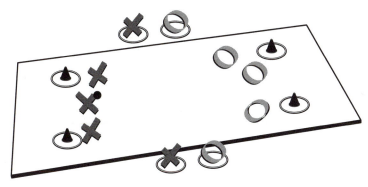

a   Starting formation.

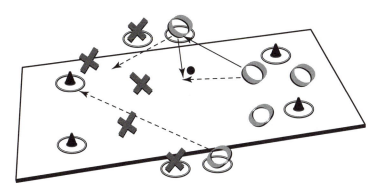

b   A defensive player intercepts the ball and makes a 1-2 pass. As soon as the turnover happens, the other outlet player is released and leads high for a fast break.

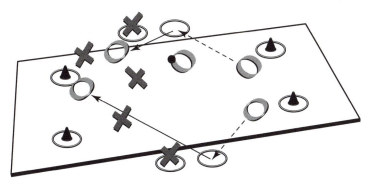

c   The other Os take up outlet positions in the hoops.

▸ Rules

Attackers

- Attackers may pass the ball in any manner, including bounce passes.
- Attackers are allowed to take a step and pivot with the ball.

- Running or walking with the ball is not permitted.
- Attackers may position themselves anywhere in front of, to the side of or behind the cones.
- One outlet player is allowed to dodge back from her waiting position to receive the outlet pass but must stay out of the playing area until she executes the one-two pass with the player who passed her the ball.
- The outlet player not receiving the outlet pass may take to the court as far forward as she likes, positioning herself to receive a long counter-attacking fast break pass.

Defenders

- Defenders must remain one step away from attackers.
- Defenders may block shots at cones with any part of the body, including the legs, but they must not strike the ball with their feet in a kicking motion.
- All interceptions result in an automatic turnover of possession.
- Defenders may not stand inside the hoops.
- Defenders may not hold on to or secure in any way the cones that constitute the goals.
- Following a turnover in a team's defensive half, defenders must make an outlet pass. This pass cannot be contested or intercepted by the opposition—it is a free pass. On receiving the pass, the outlet player passes the ball back into play (using a one-two pass) to the team-mate who passed her the ball and joins the game. The two players who did not make the outlet pass leave the game and occupy the outlet hoops near the halfway point. In this way, each team maintains only three players on the court.

General

- The ball hitting or knocking over a cone is a goal.
- After a goal the ball is turned over to the defenders, who become the attackers.

- Any ball that is thrown out of the playing area is treated as a turnover (i.e., the ball is given to the team that did not throw it out of the area).
- Each team is allowed to call two time-outs in the time period set for the game to discuss tactics.

▶ Variation

The major variation in this game concerns the contestability of the outlet pass. I suggest that with novices to the game you do not allow the outlet pass to be contested because you want players to experience as much success as possible with the game concept. However, with more experienced players, this pass could be contested.

▶ Sport Language

- Fast break
- Counter-attack
- Leading
- Defensive lines
- One-two pass

▶ Tactics and Strategies

The basic strategy of a fast break in sports is that the previously defending team moves the ball, their players or both as quickly as possible from defence to attack and in behind the team that was just attacking. In this way, the previously attacking team now has the difficult task of chasing back their opponents. The key player to achieving this tactical outcome is the player on the opposite side to the play recognizing at the moment of turnover of possession the opportunity for the counter-attack and to quickly lead forward to receive the fast break pass.

In this game, both teams must use their outlet players for either safe or high-risk counter-attacking outlet passes. When counter-attacking, it is important not to have both players back or forward, and as a general rule, the outside player dropping back for the outlet pass should be the player on whose side the opposition attack is being mounted. The player furthest from the opposition's attack should be in the attacking hoop. Positions could change frequently.

Upon getting the ball, the defensive team should look to pass to the safe outlet player. The opposition should be encouraged to retreat. This time the person who made the pass to the outlet player stays in to encourage one-two passes and the concept of support play. Also, the team now always has a forward attacking player to try to pass to. This player should lead into space and either continue a forward run or make a sudden turn and dodge back to receive the fast break pass.

Because the switch from defence to attack happens quickly, it is difficult for all the players to get forward to support the attack, but it is very important that one player works as hard as possible to catch up to the fast break player. If the fast break does not result in an easy, quick shot at the cones, then players must show patience with the ball and allow the third player to get in position to support their play.

The fast break also requires attackers to adjust how they attack. They cannot have everyone high on attack. One player must play more defensively to prevent a successful fast-breaking counter-attack. This game places a premium on fitness and mental attitude in terms of making an effort both in attack and defence.

This is quite a complex game and will take time to teach. However, the concepts are extremely important. Once they grasp them, the students will enjoy the fast-paced, high-scoring nature of the game.

▶ Attacking Skills

- Fast break
- One-two passes
- Leading to receive a pass

▶ Defending Skills

- Running defensive angles to stop the quick, long counter-attacking pass
- Attacking the outlet pass

▶ Questions

Attackers

Q: What do you call an attack that starts from defence and breaks quickly to attack?

A: A fast break counter-attack.

Q: What is the name and tactical advantage of using the quick interchange pass between the same two players?

A: The one-two pass.

A: It makes it difficult to mark the passer, and this type of passing can very quickly beat a defender.

Q: After the outlet pass, what must the opposite forward player do?

A: Lead into space to be on for a long pass.

Q: Should the most forward attacking player always run to the same place?

A: No. She should vary the lead but look for space.

Q: Can the forward attacking player influence the game even if she doesn't get the ball? How?

A: Yes, because she makes the opposition defend differently by keeping or getting a player back to defend against the fast break. Having this defensive player back provides more room in the midfield for the team in possession of the ball to move.

Defenders

Q: Of the two outlet players, which should dodge back to receive the outlet pass when one's team is defending? Why?

A: The one on the side closer to the ball, because it is the quickest and shortest outlet pass for the defenders.

Q: When some players remain on attack even when their team is defending, what is the team trying to stop the attacking team from doing?

A: It is trying to prevent the attacking team from committing all of the team to attack. This divides its resources and creates more midfield space.

Q: At a turnover, what should the most defensive attacking players do?

A: Drop back to contest the long outlet pass to the leading player.

Q: What might the most attacking player do?

A: Try to force a turnover or slow the attack down.

Q: Why is it important for the defending team to slow the opposition's attack down?

A: It gives the other defending players an opportunity to get back in defence.

Progressive (Layering) and Sliding Defence

The next group of games teaches the defensive concepts known as sliding and layering defence. The concepts are quite simple and can be used in either man-to-man defensive systems or in zone defences.

A man-to-man sliding defence in a game such as rugby typically requires the defensive players to mark inside their opposite player. The formation often results in the defensive player aligning himself with the opposite shoulder of the opponent (e.g., his right shoulder in line with the attacker's right shoulder when the attacker is moving to the defender's right). This always leaves the last attacking player with space on the outside of the playing area. But as the ball is moved across the field, the defensive players all drift or slide across in time with the passage of the ball. When it arrives at the outside player, he finds he has been squeezed to the sideline and is left with very little space to move in and only one choice—namely, to try to beat the player marking him on the outside nearest the sideline of the playing area.

To beat this type of defence, attackers need to move the ball quickly, using unexpected cutbacks against the direction of the play or having very fast players on the outside.

With zone defences, the defenders take up positions in front of their goal area. They often have one player who points the defence by confronting the on-ball attacker. If the on-ball attacker passes off to a team-mate, either the pointing defensive player slides to point at the new attacker or another defender takes that role and the previous pointing player drops back more into the defensive zone.

In a progressive, or layered, defensive system, one player confronts the attackers, usually up the field or court. The object is to slow the attack down and give team-mates time to get into position. It can also be a tactic to hurry the attackers into making a poor pass. However, as the attackers come forward, that forward defender also drops back where he progressively joins more and more defenders. In the midfield he might be joined by three or four players, but in the defensive zone all players could be involved.

The games in this section illustrate these concepts.

Splitz Attack

All students can play this simple game and learn some advanced defensive and attacking concepts. In terms of attacking, the game teaches concepts associated with the timing and splitting of attacks so that the opposition is forced to divide its defensive resources. It also introduces the concept of sacrificing one's own progress for the good of the team. These are all important lessons that can transfer to specific sports. In defence, players learn to be patient, not to chase one player, to communicate and to mark off to the side of players to try to force (channel) attackers in a particular direction. Another important concept to learn is how to layer a defence to make progress by the attackers more difficult. This game provides an early introduction to these concepts in a formal, structured but fun way.

Learning Objectives

Players will do the following:

- Split their attack
- Learn the concept of timing attacks
- Feint attacks
- Sacrifice
- Learn concepts associated with layering defence
- Channel
- Use a sliding defence

Equipment

- 18 upright cones for gates and several flat cones to designate the safe zones in levels 2 and 3
- Bibs to identify the defending players

Formation

Use the cones to lay out the court (a netball court or similar area divided into thirds) as illustrated (figure a). Six easily identified defenders (gatekeepers) stand in front of the gates to the levels. The rest of the players start outside the defined area in front of level 1.

Recipe

Six defenders stand in front of the gates to the levels as follows: One defender guards the two gates lead-ing into level 2, two defenders guard the three gates leading into level 3, and three defenders guard the four gates leading into level 4. The defenders are restricted to the areas immediately in front of the gates. They cannot go into a safe zone. They attempt to tag attackers as they try to get through the gates.

The rest of the players, the attackers, start outside the defined area. On the start signal they all try, at the same time, to progress through to level 4 (the other end of the playing area; see figure b). They must go through a gate to get to the next level. There is a safe zone in front of each level. Once they move out of the safe zone, they cannot retreat back to it but must try to get through a gate. Attackers who are tagged move to the side of the playing area.

After all the attackers are through the gates or tagged, the tagged players are counted, and that number is the defenders' score (see figure c). Play repeats, rotating the defenders' positions. At the end of a set number of games, total the defenders' scores.

Rules

Attackers

- Attackers may run and dodge to avoid being tagged by defenders.
- Attackers may not go outside the designated playing area to avoid a tag.
- Attackers may not retreat back to a safe area once they have moved out of it to try to get through a gate.
- Attackers who are tagged must go to the side of the playing area. After an attack they are counted and represent the defenders' score.

Defenders

Defenders may not tag a player in a safe area.

General

Discuss safety issues, especially the potential for people to be knocked over, and safety rules you may wish to impose. The concept of fair play is very important for the safe enjoyment of this game.

Variations

Before starting the game, the attacking players trying to get through the gates nominate a player,

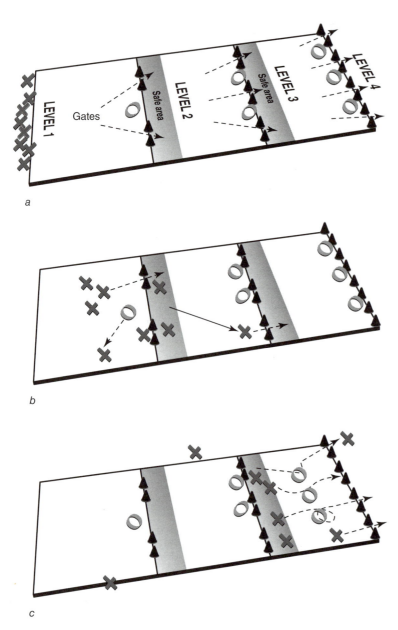

LEVEL 1
LEVEL 2
LEVEL 3
LEVEL 4
Gates
Safe area
Safe area

a

b

c

Defenders could discuss tactics for tagging more opposition players or develop attacking ploys. Concepts such as communicating, calling, sacrificing and using decoys could quickly become part of the game and discussions.

▶ Sport Language

- Split attack
- Decoy running
- Sacrificing
- Channeling
- Sliding zone defence
- Flat in defence
- Pointing on defence

▶ Tactics and Strategies

Splitting the attack and the sliding and layering defence are the key concepts associated with this game. Because there is always one more gate to get through than there are defenders, the main attacking strategy is to split the attack: when the defenders move to stop one attack, attackers launch another through a spare gate. To do this, the attackers must show patience because, although initially it looks as though the attackers have a substantial advantage, a sliding defence with good communication can make getting through to level 4 very difficult.

Key defensive concepts involve the gatekeepers into levels 3 and 4 guarding slightly off the centre line of the gates. The objective is to direct, or channel, the attack towards one gate. It is also important that these gatekeepers do not stand in a flat line or get caught up in the excitement of going for a player as they open up the gates for the other attackers. They also need to discuss how to slide across together or what their defensive formation will be. This last point is especially important for the gatekeepers to level 4.

You can manipulate the game to favour the attack or the defence by varying the distance between the gates. Initially, place the gates for entry into the levels a good distance apart to favour the attackers. Bring them closer together as the attackers learn the concept of splitting the attack and develop their timing and feel for when to run through a gate.

in writing, whom they intend to get into level 4. This encourages them to employ tactics, for example deliberately getting tagged to make it easy for the designated player to get through the gates. Encourage the defenders to try to identify the designated player. This is good practice for determining what a team is trying to do in a game.

Another variation is to introduce a scoring system, which gives 1 point to everyone who gets to level 2, 2 points to those who get to level 3 and 3 points to those who reach level 4. You could make this a competitive game by dividing the group in two.

▶ Attacking Skills

- Splitting the attack
- Feinting an attack
- Sacrificing one player to get designated players through the gates

▶ Defending Skills

- Channeling
- Off-centre marking
- Sliding zone defence
- Pointing on defence
- Communication

▶ Questions

Attackers

Q: What attacker positioning strategy at the start of the game will disadvantage the defenders?

A: Spreading out and being prepared to go through either gate.

Q: Is there an advantage to delaying entry into level 1?

A: Yes. By delaying, the attacker can see what the defender is going to try to do and put doubt in his mind about when the attack will come.

Q: How can the attackers make it difficult for the defenders once they get into level 2?

A: Again, they can spread out and fake attacks on the gates.

Q: What is meant by trying to attack while the defence is in transition, or square?

A: Attackers wait until the defenders get caught changing their relative positions of one in front and one behind. At one stage they become 'square', which gives the attackers more room in which to attack.

Q: Is it possible to fake an attack?

A: Yes, but attackers should remember that once they enter play, they cannot go back to the safe zones.

Defenders

Q: How does the placement of the cones, or gates, help the attack or defence?

A: The closer they are together, the easier it is for the defence to create congestion. The further they are apart, the more width the attackers have to move in.

Q: What does the effect of the placement of the cones, or gates, indicate about a basic strategy for defending in a game?

A: A congested, or compact, defence is much more difficult to penetrate than one that is spread out. Hence, attackers are always trying to draw out defences, and defenders are always trying to maintain a tight structure.

Q: The level 1 defender cannot stop all of the attackers. What might be his main function against the attack?

A: To slow down the attack by channeling the players in one direction and then trying to tag selected or targeted players.

Q: How can the defender at level 1 best achieve the functions listed in the previous question?

A: He can discuss with team-mates who the key attacking players are in the other team and make it difficult for those players to get through one gate and encourage them to channel through the other gate. When they see the key opposition player(s) committed to a gate, they then try and effect a tag on those players.

Q: How can two defenders defend three gates at level 2?

A: They can use a sliding zone defence by coming forward and both standing to one side of the cones.

Q: Is it best to have the defenders in a line or one player slightly forward of the other?

A: One should be slightly forward of the other; defenders should not be in a straight line.

Draw and Pass

This game continues the development of concepts associated with attackers targeting defenders and searching for overlapping attacking opportunities. Defenders are involved in trying to direct the attack in one direction and sliding across with the transfer of the ball. This game requires fundamental movements associated with catching and passing a ball while running. The restriction on the passing is that the pass must travel either laterally or backwards. These are quite complex skills, and students must be developmentally ready to undertake them.

Learning Objectives

Players will do the following:

- Learn the tactical attacking ploy of drawing and passing
- Target defenders
- Coordinate their defence
- Employ a sliding defence
- Pass a ball laterally without having it travelling forward
- Catch a ball while running forward

Equipment

- One rugby-type ball for every team of four players
- Bibs to distinguish teams

Formation

Choose a defined rectangular area such as half the length of a standard school gymnasium; the game is played across the width of the rectangle. Create three teams of four players. Teams are distinguished by wearing bibs. One team of four, the defending team, starts on one side of the gym. Two players from this team rest while the other two wait on the sideline to join the game as defenders. When the game starts, these two players come forward and attempt to defend against the four attackers for half the designated playing time (e.g., 1 of 2 minutes). They then change places with the two resting players.

The other two teams start on the opposite side of the gym. One team of four rests; the other team is the attacking team (see figure a). The four players on the attacking team spread out along their half and side of the gym. One player has the ball. The object is to get the ball to the far side of the gym without dropping it, throwing it forward or being tagged while in possession of the ball.

A simple organisation for a larger group is six teams of four players. Three teams play in each half of a gymnasium. One team rests, one attacks and one defends. Teams rotate their roles.

Recipe

On the call of 'Start', the four attackers move forward with the objective of evading the two defenders and getting the ball to the opposite side of the playing area (see figure b). They must do this without being tagged while in possession of the ball. To avoid being tagged, they may run, dodge and pass the ball, but the ball must not travel forward. In addition, they are not allowed to drop the ball or run outside the playing area with the ball.

The defenders attempt to tag a player in possession of the ball, intercept a pass or pressure a player into throwing forward or throwing a poor pass that cannot be caught.

If the attacking team runs the ball into the scoring zone on the far side, it scores a goal (see figure c). After scoring, the attackers all run back to the starting side of the gym and start another attack. They cannot start another attack until all players have returned to the start position.

If an attacker is tagged or forced out while in possession of the ball, she must stop and restart the game with a pass. All players in the attacking team must either be behind or level with the player who restarts the attack. The defenders must retreat five steps from the restart unless that takes them into the scoring zone they are trying to defend. The attackers can retreat further back if they feel they are too close to the defenders.

A dropped or forward pass also requires all four attackers to return to their starting side of the playing area to restart their attack.

The attackers have a designated time period in which to score as many points as possible (e.g., 1 or 2 minutes). The time period gives a sense of urgency to the game, and the shuttle-type running (i.e., having to run back to the start after a score, a dropped ball or forward pass) introduces the element

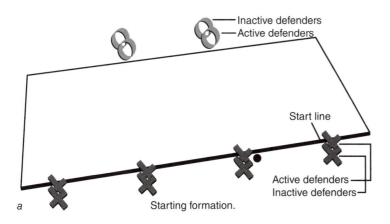

Inactive defenders
Active defenders

Start line

Active defenders
Inactive defenders

a   Starting formation.

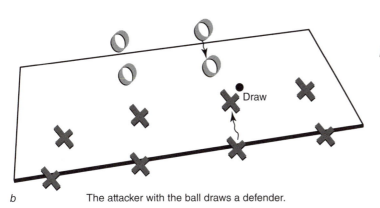

Draw

b   The attacker with the ball draws a defender.

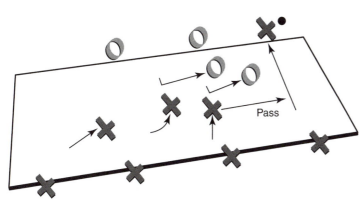

Pass

c   The attacker passes to the unmarked teammate,
who advances to score.

of fatigue. Note that the two defenders get to change with the other two players in their team halfway through the time allocated for a team to attack.

▶ Rules

Attackers

- Attackers may run with the ball within the playing area.

- Passes must be lateral or backwards.
- A forward pass requires all the attackers to return to their starting positions and restart their attacks.
- A dropped pass requires all of the attackers to return to their starting side of the playing area and start again. A new attack cannot be started until all players have returned to their side of the area.
- When an attacker is tagged in possession of the ball or forced out, she must stop and return to the point of the tag or where she ran out of the playing area. She restarts the attack from this position with a pass.

Defenders

- Defenders may only move forward from their side of the playing area when the game starts.
- For all restarts within the allocated game time, defenders may start at halfway across the playing area.
- For restarts for tagging a player or a force out, defenders must retreat five steps from the restart position.

▶ Variation

The only variation I have employed with this game is in the amount of time I allow for the attacking periods.

▶ Sport Language

- Draw and pass
- Sliding defence
- Targeting a player
- Dummy pass
- Faking a pass

▶ Tactics and Strategies

This game further develops the concepts associated with the game Eliminator in chapter 1. The difference here is that there is less congestion and the attacking and defending roles are more clearly identified. The shape of the playing area is also different. In this game, the attacking area going forward is relatively shallow, but the lateral area is quite wide. This is similar to many rugby football games in which they mount attacks within the opposition half or defensive quarter. At that point, the field area is wider than it is long. Because rules prevent players from playing in front of the ball, such games require the use of quick passing and creating overlaps or force ratios of more attackers than defenders to score points.

Attackers must try to draw defenders to positions that allow passes to an outside, unmarked player. The attackers try to make the defenders commit to trying to tag them so they cannot anticipate the timing of the pass and drift across and tag the receiver. Throwing a dummy pass is an important tactic in achieving that outcome. To do this, teams should not have the outside players carry the ball to the defenders as the only pass available is infield and of course it is predictable.

Attackers must also learn to 'run on to the ball'. Because the ball cannot be passed forward, the receivers must always start slightly behind the passers. As the pass is made, they run forward, on to the ball. If they can achieve this while running slightly faster than the passer, then the difference in speed between them and the defender who has had to slow down to make the tag on the ball carrier gives them a speed advantage against the defence.

The defenders need strategies that allow them to try to force an attack in a particular direction. As soon as they see an attack moving across one way, they have to defend inside the passer and receiver. Working together in this way ensures that the ball keeps going in that direction so that the final player receiving the ball is either tagged or forced out of play and therefore requires a restart.

The defenders attempt to slow down attacks and especially make teams restart from forward or dropped passes because this uses up the time allocated to the attackers. They also have to coordinate their changeovers with the other two defenders so the attackers do not get a chance to score an unopposed goal.

▶ Attacking Skills

- Draw and pass
- Running
- Dodging
- Running on to a pass
- Dummy, or fake, pass

▶ Defending Skills

- Recognising opponents' likely attacking options
- Reading and anticipating likely passes
- Intercepting passes
- Disrupting receivers' passes
- Forcing teams to move in one direction
- Sliding defence (i.e., marking on one side of a player and moving laterally across the playing area at the pace of the passes, thus preventing the attackers from bringing the ball back against the direction in which they are moving.)

▶ Questions

Attackers

Q: Why is it important for the inside and not outside players to carry the ball forward towards the defenders?

A: Inside players always have two passing directions available to them. The outside players can run and dodge but only pass in one direction.

Q: Where should the support players run in relation to the ball carrier?

A: They should be 2 or 3 metres (2 or 3 yd) away and slightly behind the ball carrier so the ball can be passed to them without travelling forward. They should always try to give the ball carrier two passing options.

Q: Why should the receivers learn to 'run on to the ball'?

A: By travelling faster than the passer, the receiver also gets to travel faster than the defender, and in an overlap position that should result in the attacker getting away and scoring a goal.

Q: Why should the passer delay her pass when running directly at a defender?

A: By delaying her pass, the passer draws the defender towards her, committing the defence to one attacking player so that when she makes the pass, it is very difficult for the defender to turn, chase and catch the receiver.

Q: If an outside player receives the ball and immediately runs infield, what should the attacking player immediately inside do?

A: Run behind the player moving infield, anticipating a pass. In just moving to that position and keeping that passing option a possibility, she will slow down the defence's actions.

Defenders

Q: How should the defenders start their defences?

A: They should observe who has the ball and position themselves in the spaces either side of that player but close enough to tag her if she attempts to run through that space.

Q: What is a sliding defence?

A: As the ball is passed laterally by the attackers, the defenders slide, or drift, across the playing area following the ball but not committing to trying to make a tag until the final player in the line has received the ball. In that position, one defender can make the tag while the other prevents a return infield pass.

Q: What can the defenders waiting to come into the game do to help their team-mates?

A: They can provide positive and encouraging feedback, reminding them of defensive strategies.

5-3-2 Goal!

The movement skills necessary for playing this game are quite simple, but to get even a modest proportion of the available points, teams have to pre-plan their attacking strategies and be patient in constructing attacks. For the defence, communication and cooperative play are paramount in overcoming the player number advantage held by the attackers.

Many of the previous games were structured, through both the rules and playing formations, to ensure that the desired tactical learning outcomes were achieved. Successfully playing this game requires the application of many of those tactics. However, because the employment of those tactics is not strictly structured into this game, players must decide how to use them. After playing this game, teams should be given time to reflect on the tactics they can employ both in attack and defence.

▶ Learning Objectives

Players will do the following:

- Learn how to layer their defence
- Communicate about and time possible interceptions or tags of the attackers
- Make decisions on how to defend based on the state of the game
- Learn the importance of width in attack
- Maintain depth in attack
- Employ back and around passes

▶ Equipment

- One netball (or similar) per 12 players
- Two large cones to mark a goal (a handball goal is ideal) for each game
- Bibs to identify the defending players

▶ Formation

Use a netball court or similar area divided into thirds. Create two teams of six players. The attacking team has six players on the court. The defending team has only three players on the court, one of whom is designated as the goalkeeper. The defensive players rotate on and off the court after a set number of attacks.

▶ Recipe

The attacking team has five attacks to try and score a maximum of 100 points (10 points for ten successful passes and 10 bonus points if they also score a goal). The six attackers, in possession of the ball, attempt to move through the three zones after making a set number of passes in each zone (5 then 3 and finally 2) while avoiding dropping the ball, throwing it out of play or being tagged while in possession of the ball. The attacking team cannot run with the ball. In the first zone, where the six attackers are confronted by one defender, they must complete five passes (for 5 points; see figure a). If they do, they attempt to move, also by passing to team-mates, into the second zone, where they must complete three passes (for 3 points; see figure b).

The defender of the first zone retreats to join the defender in the second zone (six on two defenders). If the attackers successfully complete the three passes, they move into the third zone, where they try to complete two passes (for 2 points; see figure c). Both defenders from zones 1 and 2 move back and join the third defender (goalkeeper) in the final zone (six on three defenders). The name of the game reflects the scoring system employed in the game (i.e., 5-3-2 plus 10 bonus points for a successful shot into the goal).

Although it might take more than 10 passes to progress to the third zone, it frequently requires several passes to move from one zone to another. A team can only score a maximum of 10 points moving through the zones. After the two passes in the third zone, a bonus 10 points can be scored if the ball is thrown between the two cones, below waist height, for a goal.

With the exception of the goalkeeper, all players, both attackers and defenders, must stay outside the goal circle marked on the netball court (see page xvi for dimensions). Only one defender may be the goalie.

The attacking team has five attempts (attacks) to score a maximum of 100 points, always starting from the first zone. New attacks occur either after a goal is scored or the defence stops the attack. After the first team has had five attacks, the teams change roles (i.e., defenders become attackers and attackers the defenders).

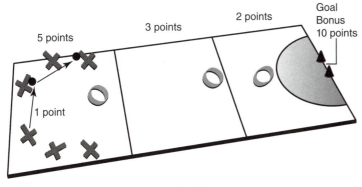

5 points

3 points

2 points

Goal
Bonus
10 points

1 point

a   5 passes, 1 defender

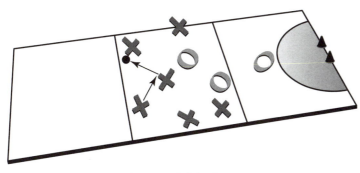

b   3 passes, 2 defenders

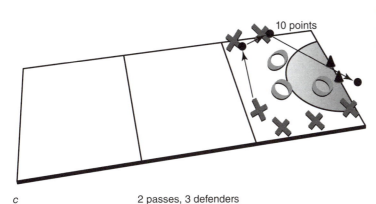

10 points

c   2 passes, 3 defenders

▸ Rules

Attackers

- Attackers move through the three zones by passing the ball. They cannot bounce pass the ball.
- Running or walking with the ball is not permitted.
- Attackers may take a step and pivot with the ball.
- Attackers must pass the ball between zones.
- Attackers may not enter the goalkeeper's area.

Defenders

- Only one defender is allowed in the first zone. Two are allowed in the second, and three are allowed in the third.
- The goalie is the only player allowed in the goalkeeper's area. The goalkeeper may also play outside of his goal area but is constrained to the final third.
- A team is only allowed one goalie.
- Defenders may be subbed after each attack (i.e., three come off and three go on).
- An attack may last until the 10 points for passing have been scored and the team has scored from a shot at goal.
- An attack is finished if the defenders intercept a pass, if they tag an attacker holding the ball, if the ball is dropped or if the attacking team puts the ball out of the playing area (e.g., misses a shot or has a pass deflected out by a defender).

▸ Variation

Restrict the time the attacking team may be in the third zone to 10 seconds. This gives the defenders a chance to be rewarded for good defence.

▸ Sport Language

- Layers in defence
- Zone defence
- Pointing on defence
- Back and around passes

▸ Tactics and Strategies

In this game the attackers are confronted with progressively more defenders. This congests the space and reduces the decision-making time. It reinforces the value of width for the attackers, and it forces the defenders to compromise between going all out for a turnover and preventing the attackers from getting the ultimate prize of the bonus points for scoring a goal.

This scenario mirrors many real-game situations in which teams layer their defence, dropping more and more players back as the opposition attacks. In sports such as football, teams often allow their opponents to pass the ball around their defensive zone with only minimal attempts at opposing their action. They do this knowing that the really important areas to defend are the midfield and their own defensive zone.

The construction of this game also reflects authentic sports in terms of attacking zone play. Because attacking zones are usually heavily congested with defenders, it is important to require the attackers to only complete two passes before undertaking the important function in this zone of trying to score a goal.

The attackers too must compromise between all-out attack and patience. Attacking teams need to be shown the advantage of passing the ball backwards rather than always forward. In this game, bonus points can be the difference between winning and losing, so setting up for and taking a shot is very important.

▶ Attacking Skills

- Back and around passes
- Maintaining depth and width in the attack
- Quick passes

▶ Defending Skills

- Communication
- Layered defence
- Zone defence
- Sliding defence
- Anticipation

▶ Questions

Attackers

Q: How do attackers need to set out their team to ensure that they can collect the relatively easy points in zone 1?

A: They should spread out and move around always trying to give the person with the ball two passing options.

Q: Before passing into the next zone, how many passing options might be advisable?

A: Two or three options should result in someone being on for an easy pass.

Q: In passing into the final zone, is there any way to position players to ensure that the receiver is not suddenly surrounded by three defenders?

A: Place two players near the target so the defenders are reluctant to move up so as to avoid a pass behind them for an easy bonus shot.

Q: Can a player perform an attacking function without actually receiving a pass?

A: Yes, by drawing opponents out of, or holding them in defence, or by blocking their access to attacking players.

Defenders

Q: In the first two zones, how can defenders position themselves to influence the direction of the pass?

A: They can make it easy to pass one way and not another.

Q: When defenders retreat from the attackers, who should do the talking in terms of organising the defence?

A: The deepest defender, because he has the best view of all the attackers.

Q: In what situations is it acceptable for defenders not to defend the first zone?

A: When the opposition is very good, when they are tired or when they are winning by lots of points.

Q: What must be the main objective of defence in the final zone?

A: To prevent the bonus points and play out time. Bonus points double the opposition's score.

Q: How should defenders set up their players to defend the goal?

A: In a triangle that points to where the ball is with the other players covering.

Q: Is it acceptable for defenders to rush out of defence in the final zone?

A: Yes, but only if they are sure they can intercept the ball or stop the attack, such as when an attacker makes a bad fumble or when pressure will put the next pass under extreme pressure.

Team Formations

When I started playing team sports, the most common line-up for players in games such as field hockey and football was 5-3-2-1 (i.e., five forwards, three halves, two fullbacks and one goalie). This attacking formation is seldom, if ever, adopted by today's teams. Teams adopt more defensive formations, looking to prevent the opposition from scoring and then using a fast break, or counter-attack, to score.

Teams also often adopt different playing formations for home and away matches. Typically, teams adopt a more attacking formation at home and a more defensive one for away matches. Teams may also change formations depending on the state of the game and their desire to score or defend a lead. To ensure spectator entertainment, some sports do not allow certain types of defences. The USA National Basketball Association did not allow teams to use zone defence from 1961 to 2001 (it was called illegal defence). The league insisted on man-to-man defence to promote more exciting player match-ups.

If you are working towards, or incorporating, parts of a Sport Education model of instruction into your teaching programme, then the next two games will provide interesting opportunities for you to apply the philosophy of that model in relation to discussing with the players the tactical advantages of the arrangement of teams and requiring the players to make decisions around those formations. In the first game, Three-Zone Pass, the nature of the game is not especially important. Your main objective should be to get players to understand the various functions of players in a game and then encourage them to adopt their own playing formations in the game.

The second game, Risk, provides a fairly typical line-up of players but introduces the element of risk in using such options as slower build-ups through the midfield or playing a longer game from the back of the playing area to the attacking third. Both games should provide plenty of opportunities to discuss team tactics and formations as suggested in the Sport Education model of instruction.

Three-Zone Pass

In many team invasion games, player positions are designated by their roles in the team. Typically, there are defensive, midfield and attacking players, sometimes called strikers. Midfield players undertake an interesting role—they are usually required to contribute to both the attack and defence. In adult- or elite-level sports, indeed the roles of all the positions become blurred, but for the purposes of an introduction to player formations, assigning specific roles to players is a useful learning process.

▶ Learning Objectives

Players will do the following:

- Learn the concept of defensive, midfield and attacking roles in games
- Learn about team formations and their associated advantages and risks
- Develop leadership skills by undertaking official positions (e.g., coach)
- Catch, throw, dodge and run

▶ Equipment

- One netball (or similar)
- Four cones to mark a goal at each end of the court (a team handball goal is ideal)
- Bibs to identify opposing teams

▶ Formation

Use a netball court or similar area divided into thirds. Create two teams of seven. Each player is assigned to a third of the court, and she must stay in that third for an agreed period of the game (e.g., a quarter). One defensive player also acts as goalkeeper (see figure a). The teams decide on their playing formations (i.e., how many players they will have in each third). Ask the players to justify their formations. A standard player formation might be 3-2-2, with one of the three being the goalie. Another might be 2-3-2, with an emphasis on controlling the midfield. Only at the end of each quarter may teams change their playing formation, that is, how many players they have in each third (see figure b).

▶ Recipe

The game starts with a goalie passing the ball into play. The opposing team attempts to score by throwing the ball into the goal at the end of the court. If cones are being used to define the goals, then the ball must go into the goal below head height. Shots must be taken from outside of the goalie circle (the shooting circle on a netball court; see dimensions in the introduction). The goalie may stop shots with any part of her body, but she must not deliberately kick the ball. The goalie is the only player allowed in the goal circle. An attacking player going into the circle results in a free throw to the goalie. A defensive player in the circle results in a penalty throw 1 metre from the goal circle.

The goalie restarts with a pass from inside the goal circle if the ball goes over the back line, including any the goalie defends over the back line or if a goal is scored. If the ball goes out, the opposing team throws it in.

The ball can be moved by running with it, rolling it, throwing it or bounce passing it. Players must stop if they are tagged while holding or running with the ball, at which point they must pass. Players have 5 seconds in which to pass. There is no limit to the number of tags a team can incur. The ball cannot be snatched from another player. The ball must be passed into each third (i.e., players cannot pass the ball from one end of the court to the other without a midfield player receiving it).

For minor violations of rules, the opposition receives a free throw. All defensive players must be at least two steps back from a free throw. A penalty throw is awarded for deliberate offences in any part of the field that are considered dangerous or reflect poor sporting behavior, or when a player deliberately offends to prevent a likely shot or goal. A penalty throw is taken by an attacker 1 metre from the top of the circle with only the goalie to defend.

To further encourage understanding of game formations, you could appoint a player to be the coach of a team. The coach's duties might include deciding on the team formation, rotating players at time-outs, ensuring all players get a chance to play in different positions and providing positive feedback on different aspects of the team's play. Players should all be given opportunities to be the coach.

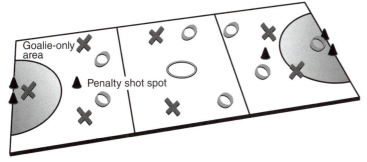

a   Starting formation.

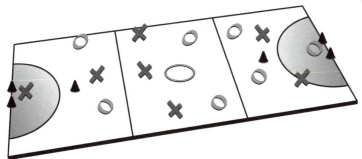

b   Teams can change their playing formation at the end of each
       quarter. Here the Os have more attackers than defenders
       and the Xs have reinforced their midfield.

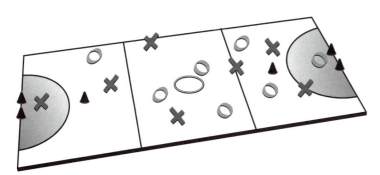

c   In this variation, players may move anywhere on the court.

▶ Rules

- Apart from kicking, field players may pass the ball in any manner including bounce passes.
- Players may run with the ball.
- Players may play only in their designated thirds until a time-out is called, and then all players are allowed to change their positions.
- Players may not enter the goalie area or mark an attempted pass from closer than two steps from the player with the ball.

- Players who are deemed to have deliberately infringed anywhere on the court have a penalty throw awarded against them. The throw is taken 1 metre out from the goalie circle. Only the goalie may defend the throw.
- Players who commit minor infringements have a free pass awarded against their team.
- A ball that goes out of the playing area is thrown in by the team that did not put it out.

Goalkeepers

- Goalies start and restart games from any ball that goes over the end line regardless of which team touched the ball last or after a goal has been scored by passing the ball to one of their players in their defensive third.
- Goalies may block shots at goal with any part of the body, including the legs, but they must not strike the ball with their feet using a kicking action.

▶ Variations

- After playing the game for some time, if you feel that the players understand the concept of defensive, midfield and attacking roles in teams, remove the thirds. Players can move anywhere except into the goalie circles (see figure *c*). This will provide an interesting insight into how well the teams retain their playing formations.
- Restrict the running: Players can run for a maximum of six steps but must then pass the ball. All other aspects of the game remain the same.

▶ Sport Language

- Team formations
- Attacking third
- Midfield
- Defensive third

▶ Tactics and Strategies

This is a simple game with an emphasis on team formations and the various player roles in each third of the court. Players need to learn that team games usually require players in all parts of the field, and that they should not put too much emphasis on one part of the game. It is important to rotate the responsibility of selecting the playing formation.

If you use players in a coaching role, encourage them to consider their formations in relation to the state of the game!

▶ Attacking Skills

- Moving to the ball
- One-two passes
- Committing a defender; then passing

▶ Defending Skills

- Verbal communication and body language. Because they have the best view of the game, it is important to encourage the goalkeepers to always be talking to their team about what the other team is doing.
- Man-to-man marking

▶ Questions

Q: Why is it important to have some players in attacking, midfield and defensive zones?

A: To give balance to the team because players need to both prevent and score goals.

Q: When might a team put most of its players in defence?

A: When it wants to defend a lead and there is not much time left in the game.

Q: When might a team put most of its players in the attacking or midfield zones?

A: When the team is losing and decides to go all out to win.

Q: What are some considerations when deciding on a team playing formation?

A: The qualities of one's own players relative to those of the opposition.

Q: What is the most important tactical factor to consider when making any changes to team formations?

A: The state of the game—that is, the score!

Risk

• • • • • • • • • • • •

The team formation element in Risk relates to the force ratio of attackers to defenders, especially in the defensive third. Here the three-to-one advantage for the team in possession of the ball demonstrates the attitude of most coaches to risk in games. Typically, coaches like a numerical advantage in their defensive third. Although it is relatively easy to keep possession of the ball with this type of ratio, it does not unduly worry the opposition because you are not in a scoring position.

In this game, players must decide between a slower but less risky build-up using the numerical player advantage in the back third and midfield or taking a risk and passing directly from the back third to the attacking third.

▶ Learning Objectives

Players will do the following:

- Learn the concepts associated with low- and high-risk play
- Understand the importance of two attackers splitting to avoid being marked by one defender
- Constantly scan possible passing options before receiving a pass
- Use back and around passes
- Understand the importance of body position relative to receiving skills so they can make quick passes to team-mates

▶ Equipment

- A supply of netballs (or similar)
- Two cones to mark a goal and lower cones to mark a goalie area if court markings don't exist. A team handball goal is ideal for this game.
- Bibs for distinguishing teams

▶ Formation

Use a tennis court or similar area or, indoors, a volleyball court divided into thirds (see figure a). Create two teams of seven—an attacking team of seven against four defenders (with three defenders who will rotate in). Position three attacking players in the back third, two in the middle third and two in

the attacking third. One defender is positioned in each third. The fourth defender is the goalie and is confined to the designated goalie area in front of the goal (see figure b). Players must stay in the thirds they are assigned to.

A game consists of at least one 3-minute inning per team. The timekeeper counts down the final 15 seconds of the game. This is designed to put pressure on both teams to either adopt risky tactics to try to snatch a win or to adopt conservative tactics to defend a lead.

▶ Recipe

The attackers start with a ball in the back defensive third. By passing the ball either through the thirds or directly to the attacking third, they attempt to score points by eventually throwing the ball into the goal. The ball can be passed back and forth between thirds. Any type of thrown pass is acceptable, although a sensible rule is to restrict the height of passes to below head height. Players may not run with the ball.

Defenders attempt to intercept, spoil or prevent passes. A defender cannot snatch the ball from an attacker. Defenders must remain one step back from an attacker. Rotate three defenders in after every minute of play (see figure c).

A goal is scored when the ball is either thrown from the attacking third into the goal or the designated area below head height and is worth 5 points. After a goal is scored, or after any turnover, the attacking team must start again from the defensive third; hence, the need for a supply of balls at the back of the defensive third. Turnovers result from dropped or intercepted passes, throwing or having the ball deflected out of the playing area, missing a shot at goal or failing to complete a risk pass.

Points are scored in three ways. Attackers can score with a successful risk pass (i.e., a pass that is successfully thrown and caught from the back to the front third), which gains the attackers 5 points. Or attackers can score with a goal: If the attackers throw the ball into the goal from the attacking third, they score 5 points. If the risk pass is not completed, the defenders receive 5 bonus points. An unsuc-

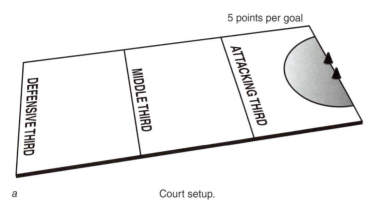

5 points per goal

DEFENSIVE THIRD MIDDLE THIRD ATTACKING THIRD

a   Court setup.

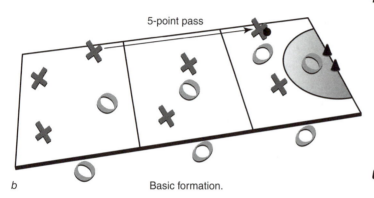

5-point pass

b   Basic formation.

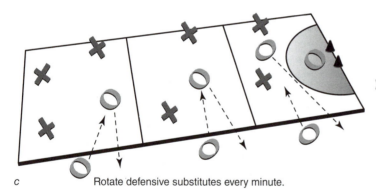

c   Rotate defensive substitutes every minute.

cessful risk pass is one that is not completed (i.e., having been thrown from the back third and is not caught by an attacker in the front third). The scorer is required to record both the attacking team's points obtained by completing successful risk passes and goals and the defensive team's points obtained by the attackers not completing risk passes.

The attacking team's score is points gained minus points lost.

▶ Rules

Attackers

- Attackers may pass the ball in any manner including bounce passes.
- Attackers may not run or walk with the ball, but they may take a step or pivot with the ball.
- Attackers may pass the ball as many times as they wish between the thirds.
- Dropping the ball ends an attack and another attack, if time permits, is immediately started from the back third.

Defenders

- Defenders must remain one step away from attackers.
- Defenders may block shots at goal with any part of the body, including the legs, but they must not strike the ball with their feet in a kicking motion.
- All interceptions or incomplete plays result in an automatic restart.

General

- A ball going out of bounds, a goal or any other turnover requires the game to be restarted in the back third with a pass.
- An inning lasts 3 minutes. A game always requires each team to have the same number of innings.

▶ Variations

- With skilled players, tagging a player in possession of the ball could also result in the completion of an attack and require another attack to be started in the back third.
- Risk also can be played by players skilled in specific sports (e.g., football and field hockey players).

▶ Sport Language

- Calculating risk
- Splitting the attack

▶ Tactics and Strategies

In this game, the attackers always have a numerical advantage of 3v1 or 2v1. They must decide whether to use a slower but safe build-up to get the ball into the attacking third for a shot at goal or the faster but high-risk direct pass from the back to the front third. The risk pass carries either a reward or a punishment (5 points to attackers or defenders) depending on its success. This is often the nature of games, and teams need to discuss and decide when the risks associated with the long pass are worth taking.

It is also important that attackers in all thirds split so that the one defender confronting them cannot mark all of them at the same time.

▶ Attacking Skills

- Calculating risk
- Communicating
- Using space to avoid one defender marking two attackers
- Keeping possession
- Accurate passes
- Throwing and catching long passes

▶ Defending Skills

- Communicating
- Channeling passes into one area

▶ Questions

General

Q: Why are 5 points allocated for the long pass from the back to front third?

A: Because of the risk involved. This is the most direct, but also most easily intercepted, pass. The risk in using it is reflected in its point value for both the attackers and defenders.

Q: When and how should players use the long pass?

A: When the risk associated with using the long pass is relatively low. For example, the potential receiver is not being closely marked and an unobstructed pass is available.

A: When a team needs to score points to catch up or extend a lead.

A: To cause doubt in the defender's mind regarding his defensive pattern. If a team only uses one attacking ploy, either short passes or the long risk pass, the attack becomes predictable and easy to defend. Using both forms of attack makes it much more difficult for the defenders.

Attackers

Q: How should the attacking team position its players in the various thirds?

A: In ways that force the defenders to only be able to mark one player at a time and therefore leave at least one easy passing option.

Q: How should attackers play if the ball isn't in their third?

A: Attackers need to be alert for passes and split to make sure one player cannot mark more than one of them at a time.

Q: What should attackers in the back third be constantly doing to see the possibility of a 5-point risk pass?

A: When they do not have the ball, they should be scanning forward to see if another attacking player is available to receive a pass. It is especially important to scan in this way immediately before anticipating receiving a pass.

Defenders

Q: How should a defender play if the ball isn't in his third?

A: He should anticipate likely attacking options and position himself in a way that allows him a chance to intercept a pass, slow down or disrupt play. This could include blocking one type of pass but being ready to intercept or disrupt the pass left open to the attackers.

════ Culminating Games ════

The games in this section allow players to fully express the many tactics introduced in the previous games. Because the games are non-specific and require a minimum number of fundamental movement skills, players can easily divide their attention between the techniques and tactics of the games. Encourage teams to employ aspects of the Sport Education model by discussing tactics, match-ups and mis-matches; practising moves or plays and employing specific attacking and defensive formations. Allow for time-outs and substitutions.

Remember that playing these games might also identify movements and techniques related to game sense that players still need to master. If that is the case, then take small time-outs from the games to undertake this practice or discussions before returning to the games. I have found encouraging goal-setting around such improvement to be a useful tool to motivate players to further develop their game performances. However, above all, organise the games to encourage participation and enjoyment.

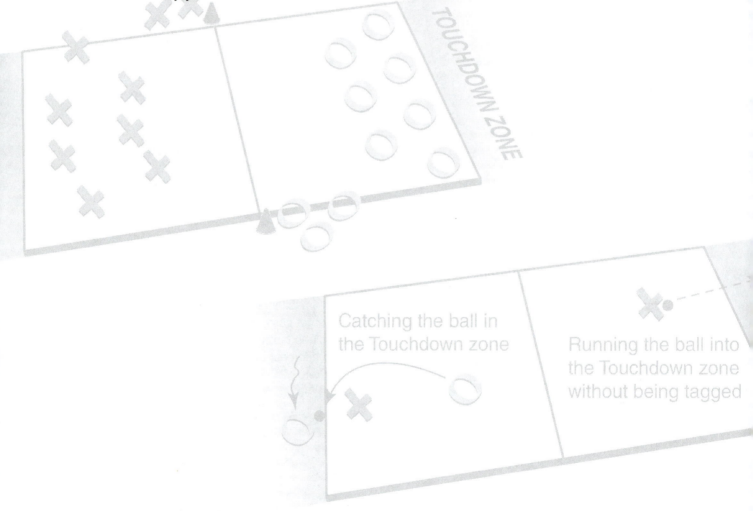

TOUCHDOWN ZONE

Catching the ball in the Touchdown zone

Running the ball into the Touchdown zone without being tagged

Touchdown

This game builds nicely from the long-pass nature of the game Risk. Students playing this game often initially overuse this long pass. However, the high number of turnovers as a result of dropped and intercepted passes soon results in a more tactical use of the long pass. This game also seems to encourage one or two players to try to dominate the play. However, teams employing sound tactics can easily overcome teams dominated by one or two players, and a more complete team game quickly emerges. The key to achieving the outcomes suggested for these games is to use the game sense approach—namely, ask the players why they are playing the way they are—and to use game scenarios as part of the playing experience. The scenarios should require whole team involvement through questioning techniques both from the teacher or coach, and within the structure or nature of the game scenario, encourage a deeper understanding of the game.

▸ Learning Objectives

Players will do the following:

- Use team formations with an understanding of the associated advantages and risks
- Understand the concept of defensive, midfield and attacking roles in games
- Develop leadership skills by undertaking official positions (e.g., coach)
- Catch, throw, dodge and run

▸ Equipment

- One small touch rugby ball, American football or similar per game
- Bibs to identify opposing teams

▸ Formation

Use a netball, basketball or similar-sized court area. Create two teams of 10 (6 or 7 on the court at any one time). Play four quarters of approximately 5 minutes. Allow 2-minute intervals between quarters.

▸ Recipe

This game is a combination of touch rugby and American football. The game starts with two opposing teams of six or seven players in their defensive halves and three substitute players (see figure a). One team throws the ball back to start the game. After the start, there are no offsides in the game.

Players may run with or pass the ball in any direction. If a player is tagged while in possession of the ball, they must stop and pass the ball. There are no limits to the number of tags a team may have. If the ball is intercepted, dropped or thrown out, or if a player runs out of the side boundaries with the ball, the ball is turned over to the opposition (see figure b). Up to two players may be substituted at any time.

Teams score a touchdown by either throwing the ball to a team-mate or running it over the end line into the scoring zone at the end of each court (see figure c). A touchdown is only scored if the ball is caught in the scoring zone or a player runs the ball into the area without being tagged. After a touchdown, a pass from behind the end line restarts play.

The team that has just scored must move back one quarter of the playing area until their opponents restart the game with a pass. After the restart, players are again free to play anywhere on the court.

▸ Rules

- At the start of the game all players must be in their defensive halves.
- A pass backwards starts the game.
- Apart from the start of the game and having to retreat out of the attacking quarter after a touchdown, there are no offsides in this game. Players may position themselves anywhere on the court.
- After a touchdown, the defensive team restarts the game with a pass in its defensive quarter.
- Players may run with the ball.
- The ball can be passed, or thrown, in any manner except as a bounce pass.
- Turnovers of possession occur if the ball is dropped, intercepted, thrown out of bounds, or if a player runs out of bounds with the ball.
- Tackles are made by tagging a player with the ball. A player tagged must stop, return to the place he was tagged and pass the ball. There are no limits to the number of tags a team may receive.

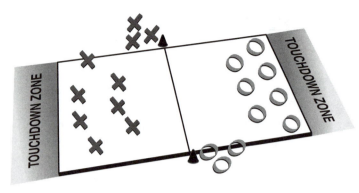

a   Starting formation.

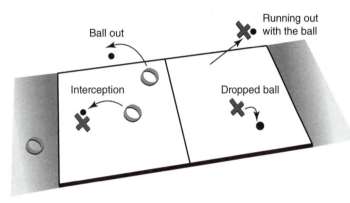

Running out
with the ball

Ball out

Interception   Dropped ball

b   Turnovers.

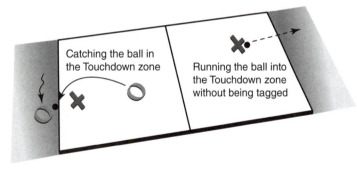

Catching the ball in
the Touchdown zone

Running the ball into
the Touchdown zone
without being tagged

c   Scoring options.

- Defenders must be two steps back from a tagged player who is attempting to make a pass.
- Each team is allowed one time-out per quarter to discuss tactics.

▸Variations

At this stage, rather than impose variations, players should be encouraged to devise their own. Some guidelines around inclusiveness or rewarding risk might be useful for the players.

▸Sport Language

- Bench
- Substitutes
- Set plays
- Defensive screen
- Leading
- Touchdown
- Manager

▸Tactics and Strategies

Touchdown is a simple game that should be played as a culmination of many of the previous games. It requires defensive, midfield and attacking players and a balance in player numbers in these positions. Note there are no formal positions or player areas in this game. It is up to the team to decide on how it will organize its player formation. Teams should be encouraged to make these decisions as a measure of their progress to understanding team formations. They should also be encouraged to consider many of the tactics from the earlier games: marking, attacking and defending, outlet passes, counter-attacking, finding space and using substitutes to ensure that their experience goes beyond just enjoying a great, fun game. This is also an excellent opportunity to appoint student coaches and managers to administer the game.

▸Attacking Skills

- Applying team formations
- Maintaining possession
- Calculating risk
- Dodging
- Running
- Throwing
- Receiving
- Finding space

▸Defending Skills

- Applying team formations
- Talking on defence to inform players of any opponent's movements behind them.
- Employing different types of defensive or marking patterns.

▶ Questions

Having been exposed to many of the tactics and strategies of attack and defence in team games, players should be encouraged to discuss and develop their own playing formations and strategies in this game. A key question to ask is whether they believe they could employ two playing formations (e.g., an offensive and defensive formation).

Teams could be given practice time to develop set plays; for example, when an attack has been stopped just short of the touchdown zone or to develop a restart or fast break play.

Encourage teams to adopt tactics such as retreating into their own half and establishing a half-court zone defence after a touchdown. This would be a good opportunity to ask the players to reflect on their experiences of playing 5-3-2 and using layering defensive systems.

Encourage students to adopt roles other than playing (e.g., coach, timekeeper, umpire, video recorder or scorer).

Specific Focus Questions for Teams

- Does your team formation reflect the rectangular shape of the playing area?

- Does your team have a set play that allows players to move quickly from defence to attack?

- If your team turns the ball over on attack, does everyone in your team understand the roles of the most forward attacking player and the most defensive player?

- Have all players been allocated playing roles that allow them to contribute to the team's performance?

- What opportunities are there for mismatches between your team and the opposition?

- How do you organise substitutions so that everyone gets to play?

- Have you a plan of how to play if you are losing and the game playing time is almost up?

- Do you have a game plan of how to defend a lead?

Rollaball

This game (reprinted from Slade, 2003) brings together many of the fundamental movements and concepts associated with attack and defence taught in the previous games. It requires the fundamental movements of running, dodging, stopping and rolling a ball. It continues the development of concepts associated with attackers making decisions relative to their attacking roles both on and off the ball. Conceptually it is quite similar to Touchdown, but it differs in that it's a goal and not line invasion game, and so zone defensive systems are more important in this game while man-to-man defence was a priority in Touchdown. Depending on whether one is going to use substitutes, teams normally consist of 4 or 5 players.

Defenders, too, are required to apply concepts associated with on- and off-ball defending. They are required to make decisions that limit the attacking opportunities of their opponents. They must communicate clearly on defence and coordinate their efforts as a team to ensure that they keep a balance between all-out defence and the opportunity to counter-attack.

▶ Learning Objectives

Players will do the following:

- Apply attacking strategies
- Apply defensive strategies
- Run and dodge
- Run and pass a ball using an underarm rolling action
- Receive a rolled ball

▶ Equipment

- Bibs to distinguish teams
- One softball or field hockey ball
- Four large cones for middle goals
- Six small cones to mark the boundaries of the playing area and the halfway point
- Four flat cones to mark corner restart positions

▶ Formation

Use a defined playing area approximately the size of a tennis, netball or basketball court. Adjust the size to suit the number and age of your players. Two teams of four or five players start the game in their own halves. The game starts with a pass-off at the halfway point.

▶ Recipe

By running with the ball or rolling it along the playing surface, teams try to score goals by getting the ball over the opponent's end line or through the goal (middle cones) on that line. This is achieved in two ways: by carrying or rolling the ball over the end line or through the goal while avoiding being tagged. For a rolled ball to count as a goal, another attacking player must receive and stop the ball behind the end line. If the pass to a player behind the end line is not stopped, it is a turnover. Players can stop the ball only with their hands.

A goal anywhere over the end (goal) line scores 1 point. A goal scored between the cones in the centre of the end line scores 5 points (see figure on page 85).

The team without the ball tries to intercept passes or force turnovers. Turnovers occur when the ball goes out over the sidelines or end lines, a player runs outside the playing area while holding the ball, a player throws rather than rolls the ball or a player stops or plays the ball with her feet.

The team that did not put the ball out rolls it in from where it went out. If the defending team puts the ball out over its own goal line, the attackers take a restart from the corner cones on the sidelines closest to the goal line. A restart following a goal takes place at the halfway point, with all players positioned in their halves. The pass-off must go back towards the team's own goal. A player may not pass the ball to herself.

A player is tackled if she is tagged while holding the ball. If tagged, she must stop and pass the ball. There are no limits to the number of tags a team can have. Players may roll the ball while running with it. When defending passes or infringements, the opposing team must retreat five steps from the player with the ball.

Players are not allowed to push opponents or deliberately play the ball with their feet. The ball must be rolled along the ground.

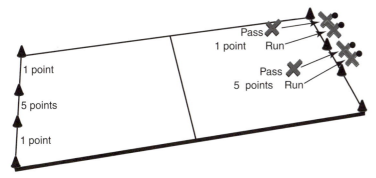

Scoring options.

Rules

- Players may run with the ball.
- Players must not run outside the playing area while holding the ball.
- The ball is passed by rolling it.
- If the ball is thrown or rolled high (i.e., off the ground), a turnover results.
- A tackle is made by tagging the player with the ball. A tagged player must return to the point of the tag before rolling the ball to another teammate. When disputes occur over whether a tag was made, the ball is returned to where the previous player last had it. There are no limits on the number of tags a team may have while in possession of the ball.
- Goals are scored by running or passing the ball over the end line for 1 point or running or passing the ball through the goal in the centre of the end line for 5 points. After a goal is scored, restarts take place at the halfway point in the middle of the playing area. The ball must be passed backwards to start the game.
- At the start of a game or after a goal is scored, all players must return to their defensive halves. Once the game is started, there are no offsides.

Variations

One variation would be to introduce rules that reinforce previous tactical concepts (e.g., requiring at least three players in a team to receive the ball before a goal can be scored). You could add that a team must make two back passes before a goal can be scored. Hopefully, such rules are not required because players should be aware of the advantages of teamwork as well as of the use of possession passes that sometimes result in the ball being passed back towards their own defensive area.

Sport Language

- Leading
- Dodging
- V-leading
- Body language
- Back and around passes

Tactics and Strategies

The main tactic addressed in this game is leading into a space to receive a pass. For this movement to be successful, players should be taught how to lead, especially V-leads. Emphasis should be on quick dodging movements. Using width and depth when one's team has the ball is extremely important. Because there are two scoring options in this game, one of which is the relatively easy pass, or run, over the end line, players must be taught to be aware of the match score so that they choose the scoring option best suited to the state of the game.

Supporting the ball carrier in this game involves not only being on for a back pass but also getting ahead of the player to receive goal-scoring passes. Teams need to understand that having players forward forces their opponents to mark these players, which provides more space for the midfield players to operate in. Emphasise to players the importance of what they do when they are not in possession of the ball.

In defence, a combination of zone and man-to-man marking is required. In the first instance, it is important to defend the centre goal because it is worth 5 points. However, if one has sufficient players defending, this can be achieved with a sliding zone defence while also trying to prevent the 1-point goals through man-to-man marking.

Attacking Skills

- Maintaining possession
- Running and dodging
- Disguising the intention to pass
- Leading into space to receive a pass; using a V-lead
- Rolling and passing accurately and especially judging the force to apply to the ball
- Using body language to indicate the intended direction of, or where to receive, a pass
- Receiving and stopping a rolling ball

▸Defending Skills

- Pyramid zone defence
- Sliding defence
- Intercepting passes
- Anticipating player movements and likely passes
- Employing a mixture of zone and man-to-man defence
- Recognising opponents' likely attacking options
- Disrupting receivers' passes

▸Questions

Attackers

Q: To provide passing options for their team, what are some basic movements attackers can make?

A: They can spread out so that they provide wide and deep passing options.

Q: Why is it important for at least one team-mate to remain behind the person with the ball

A: If the person with the ball is tagged, she then has the option of passing the ball backwards. Having a player there ensures that this can happen quickly.

Q: What is a back and around pass, and when should a team use it?

A: A back and around pass means passing the ball back from an attack and then around or across the playing area to attempt to go forward down the other side. An attacking team should use this pass when it finds its way forward down one side of the playing area blocked by the opposition. Rather than continue in that direction or risk a low-percentage pass, the team stops the forward attack, passes the ball back and around its defensive area and attacks down the other side.

Q: Why are short dodging movements, coupled with appropriate body language, important attacking skills?

A: The sudden, unexpected dodge provides a short time away from the marker in which to receive a pass. Long, steady movements are easy to anticipate and therefore mark. The body language of the receiver should reveal to the passer the player's actual intended movement direction. One expression of the use of body language is to indicate to the passer you want to receive the ball on your left. However, to confuse your defender you make a quick movement to your right before suddenly returning to your left—the direction you had always intended to move in to receive the pass.

Defenders

Q: After a turnover in the attacking half, what should the most forward of the previous attackers attempt to do now that she is a defender? What does that give her team-mates time to do?

A: This player should now try to tag the opposition player with the ball, forcing her to pass the ball from a deep defensive position, which could result in an interception while she is still in their attacking area. Alternatively, they could force the ball carrier to run towards the sideline to cut down her passing options. Defensive work by the foremost attacker turned foremost defender as a result of a turnover of possession gives the other team members time to retreat and set up their defence and slows down any fast breaking counter attack.

Q: After tagging a player, should the tagger continue to mark the tagged player, or move off to mark someone else?

A: It depends. In the defensive half, the player should mark the player to put pressure on the accuracy of her pass. In the attacking third, the player should perhaps leave her and try to mark potential receivers and force a turnover.

Q: Why is the centre goal worth 5 points?

A: The centre goal is much easier to defend, so scoring there requires more skill or tactical ability, which is reflected in the score value.

Q: What would be the main priority for a defender left by herself to defend an attack she cannot stop?

A: She should try to prevent a 5-point goal. If a defender knows she cannot stop a score, she should try to minimise the points the opposition will receive (i.e., give up the 1-point goal but do her best to prevent the opposition from scoring a 5-point goal).

3

Applying TGfU to Teaching Badminton, Basketball and Netball

This chapter illustrates the potential of the Teaching Games for Understanding (TGfU) instructional methodology to promote game learning in specific sports. To illustrate this potential, some of the game fundamentals, tactics and declarative knowledge of the sports of badminton, basketball and netball are taught. To demonstrate the flexibility of this teaching methodology, the

TGfU can enhance the instruction of netball and countless other games.
© Peter Cade/Stone/Getty Images

examples in this chapter are aimed at learners at different stages of developing competence in the games. In the netball example, the learners are assumed to be absolute novices to the game—first-time players. In badminton the players are novices, while in the basketball example, the players are assumed to have already developed some of the game's fundamental techniques. The examples also demonstrate how the TGfU approach can motivate students to want to play sports.

The badminton sequence provides an introduction to playing doubles. With the basketball games, I assumed that the players have already mastered basic dribbling, passing and shooting skills, and you are looking to develop their understanding of zone defence and how to play against it. In the netball examples, I assumed that players do not even know the names of the positions in the game, and so I structured the methodology to illustrate an approach for teaching basic declarative knowledge about rules, positions and restarts in this sport.

Because the teaching sequences in this section are only illustrations of the potential use of the TGfU methodology, thorough descriptions of all aspects of the games are not included. Gaining extensive content knowledge about these games is your responsibility. However, your previous experience from the earlier sections of this text will have prepared you to capitalise on the many opportunities to ask questions of the players regarding game tactics that occur naturally from the learning sequences in this section.

The games in this chapter also expose players' technical deficiencies. However, if the players are enjoying the game and to some extent achieving the outcomes of the game, do not be overly concerned with technique. In my experience, sooner or later players will seek help for improving their technique. When they seek or require technique development, you will find that games in this chapter provide many opportunities to improve technique within the context of games. The games also provide opportunities for students to develop a deeper appreciation of rules and to extend their game understanding by giving them officiating responsibilities.

I have not included specific assessment activities with these applications of the TGfU methodology to badminton, basketball and netball. However, it is vital that players receive feedback and assessment on their development. Before you use the ideas presented in this section with your classes, I advise you to read chapter 5 on assessment for ideas on how to develop authentic assessment for use in game instruction.

BADMINTON

This TGfU introduction to playing doubles badminton starts with a game that teaches players the basic tactics of badminton. Because badminton is played on a narrow, rectangular court with a high net, the basic strategy is to alternate between playing the shuttle just over the net (a short game) and to the back of the court (a long game).

The next modified game is used to teach players how to recognise and anticipate player movements based on the angles created by having to play a shuttlecock over a net and keep it within the confines of the court. The game that follows prepares players for positional changes on the court and teaches the footwork necessary to do so successfully.

A specific game starting sequence is then adopted to teach a doubles serve, a response and a positional change before allowing for open-skill play. A final game teaches the movement associated with retrieving the shuttle and moving back to the centre of the court.

Note that this chapter offers only a sequence of learning and not specific lessons. It is up to you to decide how much time you want to devote to, or what content you want to include in, each lesson. The lesson sequence may take you three or five lessons to complete. Make that decision based on the characteristics of your class.

You must decide the amount of time your students spend in the modified games, when to move them from modified to authentic badminton equipment and how to use basic hitting drills. I use the modifications in short bursts of activity before allowing novices to use authentic equipment in modified or actual games of badminton. I have found this approach ideally suited to badminton because, although the game at an elite level is extremely fast, requiring fit and agile athletes with both power and touch, it is also a wonderful game that novices can play with a modicum of technique and employ the basic tactics of the game. Used sparingly, this TGfU approach can motivate and teach novices the tactics and strategies of badminton and quickly get them playing the game like experts.

Following are the learning outcomes for this doubles badminton sequence:

Tactics

- Playing long and short in badminton
- Developing court craft by recognising and responding to playing angles
- Doubles side-by-side and front-and-back playing formations

Techniques

- Overhead shot
- Short shot
- Drop shot
- Doubles serve

Fundamental Movements

- Rotational movement patterns used in doubles
- Movement patterns for retrieving shots

Declarative Knowledge

- Basic serving and scoring rules

Basic Play: Short and Long

The initial learning outcomes for the badminton learning sequence are as follows:

- Learning the long and short nature of badminton
- Learning restart rules
- Learning the basic scoring system

Lob Pass

▶Equipment

Two volleyballs per court

▶Formation

There are four to six players per court. Divide the court in half longitudinally with two players on each half. Play is confined to each side of the court.

▶Recipe

The object of the game is for the players to learn the short and long nature of badminton. Standing behind the service line and using a two-handed underarm throwing action, one player throws the ball over the net into the opposite playing and service receiving area (see figure 3.1). The players get points by getting the ball to land on the floor on the opponent's side of the net. The ball is always thrown with a two-handed action, and the initial direction of the throw must be upwards. They should alternate the serving regardless of who scores a point. You can determine the play-up to score (i.e., the first person to score 3, 5 or 7 points is the winner). If you are playing 3 players per half court, rotate the third player in after one player reaches the set score. Ensure that both players get the same number of opportunities to play the game.

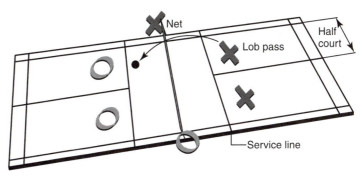

FIGURE 3.1 Lob Pass setup and play.

▶Tactics and Strategies

It soon becomes obvious to the players that to get the ball to land on the opposite side of the net, they either have to throw it to the back of the court or just over the net to the front of the court. This illustrates, of course, the long and short nature of badminton.

Players should also be learning the badminton scoring system at this stage and rules relative to serving the minimum distance.

Have your players play Lob Pass until you believe they have a good appreciation of this basic tactical approach to playing badminton.

Introducing Equipment

When you are satisfied that players have a firm grasp of badminton basics from Lob Pass, replay the game with badminton equipment—half-court badminton. The formation remains the same as in Lob Pass with one player in each longitudinal half of the court on both sides of the net. Playing in one half of the court, players try to get the shuttle to land on the floor on the opposite side of the net. At this stage, avoid all hitting instructions and just observe the players. It will become obvious who does and who does not need assistance to hit the shuttle. The techniques you will most likely see will be associated with attempted clearing, drop and smash shots.

Underarm and Reverse Backhand Serve

Teach your students the basic underarm and backhand serve. Be sure to teach them that the rules about serving in badminton state that the head of the racquet must be below the wrist, and the shuttle must be hit upwards and over the net (i.e., they cannot serve in the manner of a tennis serve). Spend only a brief period of time teaching these serves before returning to the previous half-court badminton games. Back in these games, ensure that players start each point with a serve, which puts the serve into a game context.

Overhead Clearing Shot

Observing the half-court badminton game, you will see that the players instinctively try to play an overhead clearing shot in order to play long. This is your teaching opportunity. Depending on the techniques you observe, either provide individual instruction or briefly stop the whole class and give a demonstration of the overhead clear. Show the grip and movement sequence but quickly return to the game to keep the learning within the context of the modified half-court badminton game. At this stage of instruction, do not be overly concerned with the technique, but focus on reinforcing the tactical outcomes associated with playing short and long.

Encourage the players to play cooperatively by suggesting a number of consecutive hits or a specific time period (e.g., 10 to 20 hits, or 30 seconds to 1 minute). Encourage them to hit the shuttle as hard as they can, gradually moving them back from a half- to a full-court position.

Hitting the shuttle as hard as they can allows players to recognise whether they have the technique to achieve the desired tactical outcome of this shot. It is my experience that players who cannot hit, or clear, the shuttle to the back of the opponent's court will seek assistance on how to improve their technique to achieve that tactical outcome. Within the philosophy of the TGfU approach, this is the teaching moment in which to introduce technique to those players.

Overhead Drop Shot

The overhead drop shot is an overhead clearing shot with a slower racquet action. Instead of hitting the shuttlecock to the back of the opponent's court, the player returns it to the front with the intention of barely clearing the net. Note that this shot often requires the player to disguise the action. Demonstrate the shot, and then send the players back to continue playing half-court badminton.

To encourage the use of the drop shot, modify the scoring system of the basic game so that any point won through the use of the drop shot scores 2 points. You may have to change the play-up to score to accommodate this component of the game.

Reading Playing Angles

When teaching players to read playing angles in badminton, the main desired learning outcome is that they learn court craft by recognising and responding to playing angles. You can use two activities from chapter 1 to help with this—One Bounce and Rotation Catch.

One Bounce

Place players in groups of three to play One Bounce (see page 11). Remind them of the learning outcomes. Once they are playing, use the time to set up nets for a transfer game of a similar shape (i.e., Rotation Catch).

Rotation Catch

Have students play Rotation Catch for basic rules and playing concept (see page 17). After you have referred to that game, you will see that in applying it to badminton I have slightly modified the game structure.

▶ Equipment

- Two strips of paper and two clothes pegs per badminton court, volleyball or similar ball
- One badminton racquet per player plus shuttles

▶ Formation

Using clothes pegs or something similar, attach two strips of newspaper to the net to replicate the cone placements used in the game One Bounce. Three players are on each side of the court.

▶ Recipe

Play starts as in the basic introductory badminton game by throwing the ball over the net with an underarm action lob to the opposition. The ball must travel the minimum service line distance. It must pass over the net between the pegged strips of newspaper. The player who throws the ball to the opposition rotates out of the game towards the back of the court, and the next player in the team comes forward to receive the return throw from the opposition. Figure 3.2 shows the set-up and play.

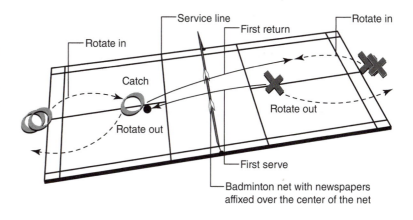

FIGURE 3.2 Rotation Catch set-up and play.

▶ Rules

- The ball must pass between the boundaries defined by the strips of paper.
- The ball must always travel the minimum service line distance.
- The ball must be played within the doubles service area (i.e., within the back and wide service lines).

▶ Tactics and Strategies

The purpose of this game is to teach players to anticipate the likely returns of the opposition based on where they are standing on the court considering that they have to throw the ball in the zone defined by the strips of paper.

This game requires that players anticipate not only the likelihood of a short or long return but also the angle of the return.

This provides an opportunity to instruct the players in the four Rs of the net game. (I first heard this four-Rs explanation of a playing sequence for net games from T. Hooper at the Third International TGfU Conference, Hong Kong, 2005.)

Recognise: See where the opponent is and recognise his returning options.

Respond: Move to a position on the court that allows you the best chance of receiving that return.

React: When the return shot is made, react by moving to intercept the ball or shuttlecock and return it in a manner that disadvantages your opponents as much as possible.

Recover: Because you are in a team, recovery is merely rotating out of the way. If you were playing singles, you would recover to a position on the court that would allow you to best observe the opponent and prepare to respond to his possible reactions.

The purpose of the restricted passing area which exaggerates the returning angles is to help players learn to anticipate the return of their shots.

Have players play for a suitable amount of time, for example, 5 to 7 minutes, and then reintroduce the authentic badminton equipment. They now play the game the same way, but using badminton racquets and shuttlecocks.

Adapted, by permission, from T. Hooper, 2003, "Four R's for tactical awareness: Applying game performance assessment in net/wall game," *Journal of Teaching Elementary Physical Education* 4(2): 16-21.

Serving and Receiving, Playing Systems and Rotation

In this sequence, players will learn components of the following:

- Serving and receiving in doubles badminton
- Playing systems, front and back or side by side in doubles badminton
- Rotation movements involved in doubles

Teach players the rules regarding serving in doubles badminton. Set up as for doubles (four players on each court; substitutes may be rotated in at your discretion). Using a volleyball, students play the first game, Lob Pass, but now as in doubles badminton. Use this game to teach the rules of doubles badminton regarding playing area and service rotation.

Have them play until you are satisfied with their understanding of the rules. Introduce again the badminton equipment and have them continue the games.

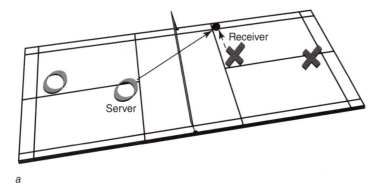

a

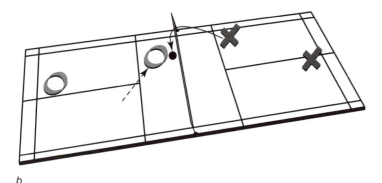

b

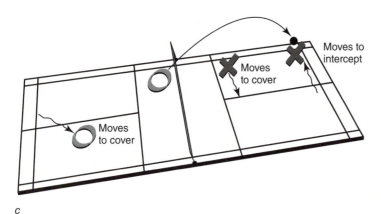

c

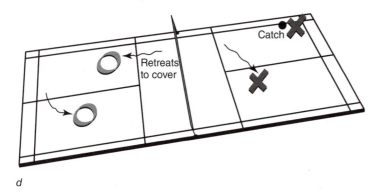

d

FIGURE 3.3 Each rally must begin with the same sequence: shot 1 (*a*), shot 2 (*b*), shot 3 (*c*), and shot 4 (*d*).

Intergame Movements

In this sequence, players learn the movements associated with changing sides while rallying in badminton.

Four players prepare to serve as in a game of doubles badminton except they will throw and catch a volleyball. To create the feel for this movement, you will prescribe the first four movements of each rally, starting with the serve as the first shot. After the fourth shot, play is open and the players may play as they wish.

- *Shot 1.* The first server serves the volleyball wide and short towards the outside doubles boundary line (see figure 3.3*a*).
- *Shot 2.* The first receiver catches and throws the ball short over the net straight in front of where the ball was received (see figure 3.3*b*).
- *Shot 3.* The server follows her serve and catches the short drop shot. Her partner moves across to the other side of the court from where the serve was made (see figure 3.3*c*).
- *Shot 4.* The first server, having caught the ball, lobs the ball in a straight line over the first receiver's head, to the back of the opponent's court. The partner of the first receiver moves across and catches the ball. The first receiver moves to the other half of her court (see figure 3.3*d*). Play on!

This sequence results in all players changing from the side of the court they occupied when the game started. The use of the volleyball makes this movement sequence achievable and quite accurate. The objective is to help players understand the need to change places frequently in this game.

Once the players appear to be performing the movement well, revert to using the badminton equipment but maintain the start sequence.

Retrieving a Shot and Returning to Position

In this sequence, players learn how to retrieve a shot and return to the T, or centre of the court, as well as the footwork and movement action required for retrieving a low shot over their heads.

Four players are on each court. Two players on one side are feeders, and two on the other side are retrievers. The second retriever stands off to the side of the court waiting his turn (see figure 3.4a). The first retriever starts on the centre line about one step back from the minimum service line. The two feeder players position themselves near the front of their court (i.e., on the other side of the net).

The feeder with the volleyball lobs the ball in a high arch over the retriever towards the back of the court on his dominant, or forehand, side. The retriever turns, takes an appropriate number of steps and reaches out and catches the ball with one or two hands. He immediately throws the ball back over the net and returns to the start position (see figure 3.4b). One of the feeders catches the ball and returns it to the same place (see figure 3.4c).

To ensure the retriever has time to get back and catch the ball and return to the T, the feeders should lob the ball quite high. The feeders should not make it impossible for the retriever to reach the ball. The idea is to ensure that the retriever has to take two steps and then reach out with a third step, catch and return the ball and immediately return to the centre of the court. Retrievers change places after a set number of retrieves (e.g., five) or when they are fatigued. Both teams have turns at being retrievers and feeders.

Next, repeat the activity using the badminton equipment. Note that this retrieving shot is played after the shuttle has dropped below head height. I use the analogy of 'scooping out ice cream' to provide a verbal picture of the shot's requirements. Anticipate that students may not play the activity as well with badminton equipment because they might not have the requisite techniques. As a teacher, you have to recognise what is required in terms of specific technique instruction. Provide the instruction but do not spend too long on it. Return them to the game and encourage them to use the techniques within the context of the game. Encourage the footwork associated with the retrieve shot.

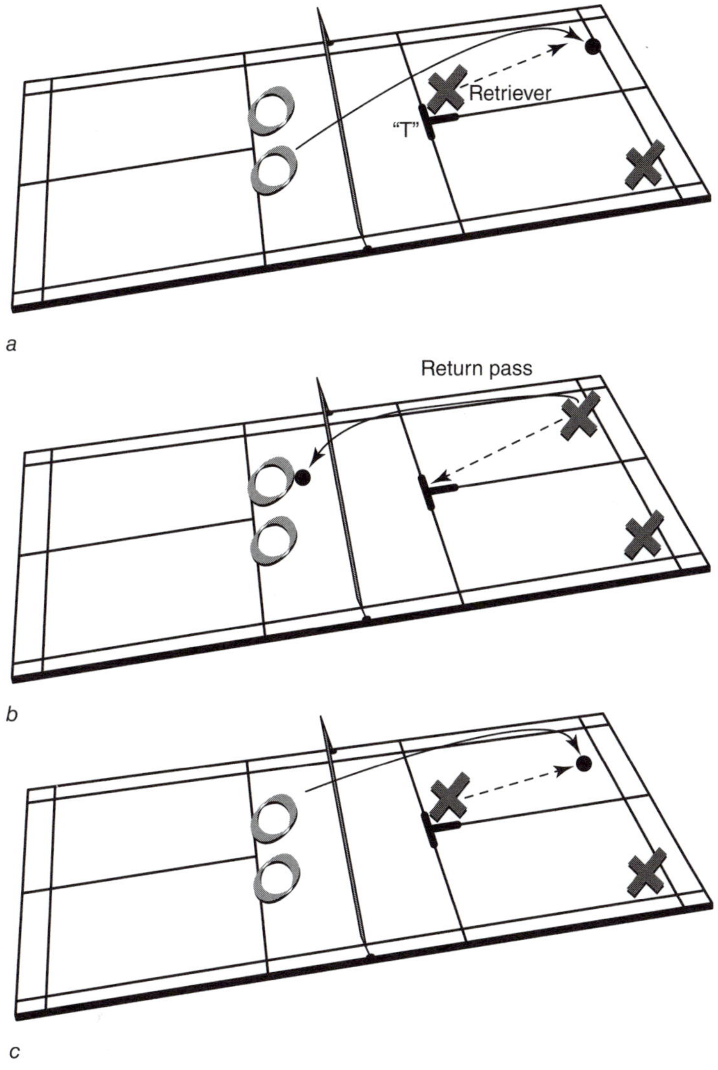

Playing Systems

The desired outcome of this learning sequence is for players to play doubles badminton using the side-by-side and front-and-back systems (see figure 3.5).

Instruct players in the basics of playing side by side and front and back. A visual demonstration either on a white board, on court or a video can be used to illustrate the formations. Players return to the court and decide which formation to try first. Using the volleyball, they play doubles badminton, experimenting with both playing systems until they feel comfortable with each system.

Reintroduce the authentic badminton equipment and allow the players to enjoy a game. Encourage them to use a playing system and evaluate how they enjoy the system.

Conclusion

There is much to cover in this sequence of instruction. What is important, though, is that you set the pace of learning based on your understanding of your class. You do this too in relation to modifying the games and introducing authentic

FIGURE 3.4 Set-up and sequence for practicing retrieving a shot and returning to position.

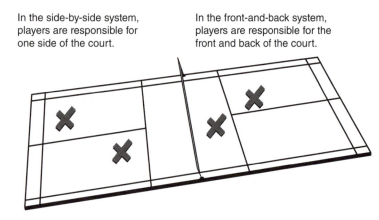

In the side-by-side system, players are responsible for one side of the court.

In the front-and-back system, players are responsible for the front and back of the court.

FIGURE 3.5 Doubles badminton playing systems.

equipment. At the heart of this introduction to doubles play in badminton is the philosophy of allowing players to explore and discover the basic tactics and strategies associated with this game and, at an introductory level, to play and enjoy the sport of doubles badminton.

BASKETBALL

For a number of reasons, basketball zone defence is a good tactical defensive system to teach in a physical education context. First, it is relatively easy to explain either through diagrams on court demonstrations or video footage. Second, the focus on the cooperative team function in zone defence takes the pressure off less skilled players who will always be in a general physical education class.

Two common zone defence systems are the 3-2 and 2-1-2 systems. The 3-2 system has three players positioned at the front of the keyhole and two defenders closer to their goal (see figure 3.6a). This system looks very like the zone defence that players are forced to play in the games in chapter 2: Zone Defence, Outlet and Fast Break. Indeed, if employing a zone defence, the 3-2 system is best suited for a fast break counter-attacking style. The 2-1-2 system has two players at the front of the keyhole, a middle player and two defensive players under or near their defensive goal (see figure 3.6b).

In this example of applying TGfU principles for teaching zone defence in basketball, the 3-2 system is employed. However, you may employ whatever zone defence system you prefer.

This example of applying the TGfU methodology targets a class in which the students may have been taught some of the fundamentals of basketball. I have assumed that you have covered dribbling, passing and shooting, especially the set shot, and you are looking to explain some of the defensive tactics employed in basketball, while still giving the players opportunities to practise many of the techniques of the game—namely, dribbling, passing and goal shooting. Some of the activities from earlier chapters are used here for that purpose.

Learning outcomes for this zone defence sequence include the following:

- Understanding the concept of zone defence
- Demonstrating a sliding zone defence
- Learning the counter-attacking strategy of an outlet pass
- Having opportunities to practise fundamental basketball skills and attacking strategies in a modified game environment

The following equipment is needed for the activities in the sequence:

- Basketballs
- Four cones
- Eight hoops
- Bibs to distinguish teams

Divide the class into teams of five and reteach the games from chapter 2, Zone Defence (page 52) and Outlet (page 55).

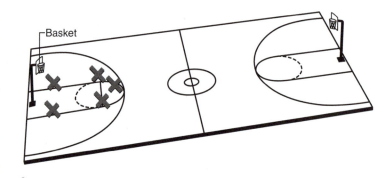

a

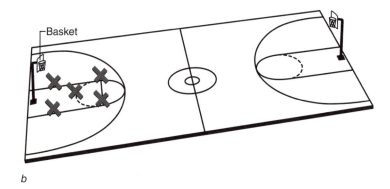

b

FIGURE 3.6 Two common zone defence systems: 3-2 (*a*) and 2-1-2 (*b*).

Zone Defence

You might wish to substitute the basketball for a volleyball in this game to prevent injuries.

Set up the formation to play Zone Defence (page 52) across the gym. With teams of five, you will have players on the sideline observing. Your objective for those players is to direct their observations at the defensive structure forced on the teams by having to defend two goals with three players. Focus their attention on what the defenders do if the ball is passed across the goals from one side to the other. Also comment on the similarity between the natural defence in this game and the 3-2 zone defence system used in basketball.

This is an especially good time to introduce time-outs and substitutions. Rotate the sideline players into the role of coach or manager. Require them to call substitutions and time-outs in which they must offer at least one piece of advice for their team.

Outlet

Set up formation for playing the game Outlet across the gym and have your students play this games (page 55). If you have only five in each team, then you will not have any players sitting out. If you have more than five per team, use the same teaching strategy you used in the previous game—namely, have the players who are sitting out look at the game strategies and call time-outs and substitutions. Once you are satisfied that the players understand the sequence of the game, move to set up the new game, Continuous Outlet.

Continuous Outlet

In authentic games, the game does not stop after a team has tried unsuccessfully to score a goal. Nor is that team given the ball back and told to try again. Indeed, the team's lack of success invites the opposition to counter-attack. In many traditional skill practices, this authentic scenario does not happen. For example, an offensive team practising goal shooting does not suffer the consequences, as it does in an actual game, of not successfully completing the shot. In Continuous Outlet, the game continues after both successful and unsuccessful shots. Defenders move to attack, and attackers become defenders. Although the game does not exactly mirror the actual game of basketball, the modifications provide opportunities to practise aspects of the defensive structure and playing against a zone defence.

▶ Equipment

- One basketball and basketball court
- Four hoops
- Bibs to distinguish teams

▶ Formation

Two teams of five, one at each end of a basketball court, set up as for the game Outlet on page 55—that is, three defenders on the court and two outlet players in hoops standing on the edge of the court close to halfway. The three defenders on the court must play within the 3-point scoring line. Ideally, they should set up on the keyhole as for the 3 in the 3-2 zone defence system of basketball. They must not advance out of this area—even in pursuit of a loose ball. A third team of five players starts in the middle of the court with the basketball (see figure 3.7a).

▶ Recipe

The middle team attacks one end of the court playing 5v3. Their objective is to score a goal. The defending team has to use a zone defence. The 5v3 ratio of attackers to defenders gives the attackers plenty of opportunities to construct their attack, get players in position and use their basic dribbling, passing and shooting skills without too much pressure from the opposition. Confining the defenders to within the 3-point shooting zone also gives the attackers time to construct and reset attacks.

Depending on your emphasis, you might want to modify the scoring system. For example, you may restrict the use of 3-point shots and layups. However, you may decide that goals scored from within the keyhole score double points (4).

If the attackers score a goal, they keep the ball, immediately turn around and attack the defenders at the other end of the court (see figure 3.7b). As long as they keep scoring, they occupy the middle of the court and continue to be attackers alternating the ends they attack.

If the defenders intercept the ball from a pass or rebound (i.e., achieve a turnover), they are allowed, without opposition from the attackers, to make the outlet pass to one of their players standing in the hoops on the side of the court. That player inbounds the ball, and she and the other outlet player on the other side of the court join the three players from their team who were the on-court defenders. This team now becomes the middle court team and commences an attack against the team at the other end of the court. The previously attacking team takes up the defensive role of three defenders and two outlet players at the end of the court they had just attacked and where they turned the ball over.

In this way the game is continuous with teams attacking, defending or moving from defence to attack.

This game requires the use of a zone defence and an outlet pass. It is not possible to play it without

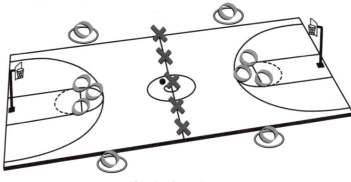

a Starting formation.

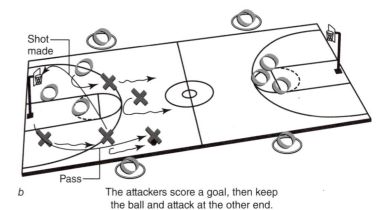

b The attackers score a goal, then keep the ball and attack at the other end.

FIGURE 3.7 Starting formation for Continuous Outlet (*a*); the attackers score a goal, then keep the ball and attack at the other end (*b*).

achieving those outcomes. However, it is important that you draw attention to the strategic concepts associated with these tactics. It is up to you to decide which attacking strategies (e.g., penetrating the keyhole and passing out for a set shot, taking the ball into the corner and then passing out and around, timing a lead into the keyhole to receive a pass and shoot and others) to emphasise.

Conclusion

It is generally assumed that a coach or teacher requires extensive content knowledge relating to basketball in order to bring out the various possibilities presented by the introduction of zone defences or how to play against such a defensive system. However, if you have only a modicum of knowledge of basketball but understand invasion games, the structure of Continuous Outlet offers

the reasonable observant teacher numerous teaching opportunities related to both the tactics and techniques of this sport.

NETBALL

Netball is a game that so strictly defines the players' roles and movements that players wear bibs that identify their positions. Players start the game in set positions with opposition players marking them man-to-man. In this game no player is allowed to cover all parts of the court; only two players can score goals, and only two players can guard against their goal shots. This has led to most teams playing man-to-man defensive systems. Also, because players may not take more than one step with the ball, players use quick passing and dodging movements off the ball to evade opponents.

In this example of the application of the TGfU methodology to a sport, the assumption is that the players have not yet learned the court positions and declarative rule knowledge related to offside (i.e., where they can move on the court and how to start and restart the game).

Learning outcomes for this netball sequence include the following:

- Knowing the player positions, the names of those positions and the offside rule
- Understanding what constitutes stepping, foul or dangerous play
- Knowing how to start a game of netball
- Understanding how to restart a game of netball after the ball has gone out of play
- Knowing how to restart a game after a simultaneous infringement between two players

Experience has taught me that knowledge of player positions and basic rules relating to offside, stepping and contact infringements need to be taught before moving into restarts.

Passing Competition Relay

▶Equipment

- Netballs, at least 5 or 6 per team
- Bibs for distinguishing teams

▶Formation

Depending on class size and facilities, this activity can be set up with one or two teams per court. Place the players in the set netball positions. Figure 3.8 shows positional names and court movement restrictions.

▶Recipe

Briefly explain the player positions in netball. Explain the positional movement restrictions and stepping rule. Place players in these positions on court. Have the players pass the ball up and down the court, starting with the goalkeeper. As players receive a pass, they call out the name of their position (not the player's name) they are passing the ball to. As soon as he has passed the ball, the player moves to the next position on the court. When the goal shooter receives the ball, he shoots a goal and then runs with the ball back to the start position (i.e., the goalkeeper). To keep this game flowing you need approximately 10 players per team.

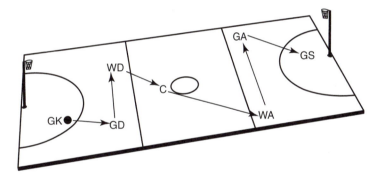

Position	Game function	Court movement restrictions
Goalkeeper (GK)	Defends against goal shooter	Defensive third of the court
Goal defence (GD)	Defends against goal attack	Defensive two-thirds of the court
Wing defence (WD)	Defends against wing attack	Defensive two-thirds of the court excluding the shooting circle
Centre (C)	Defends and attacks against opposition centre	All of the court excluding the shooting circle
Wing attack (WA)	Supports attack and is defended by wing defence	Attacking two-thirds of the court excluding the scoring circle
Goal attack (GA)	Supports attack and shoots goals; is defended by goal defence	Attacking two-thirds of the court including the scoring circle
Goal shooter (GS)	Primary goal shooter; defended by goal keeper	Attacking third including the goal circle

FIGURE 3.8   Positional names and court movement restrictions for netball.

Repeat the activity (i.e., call out the position she is passing to but also have the players state the positional movement restrictions as to where she can move on the court without being offside).

Make this game a relay competition. Start the ball with the goalkeeper; the ball must be passed to each player to arrive at the goal shooter. The goal shooter must score a goal. Once a goal is scored, the ball is passed in reverse order back to the goalkeeper. The relay finishes when the ball is in the hands of the goalkeeper. Players must receive and pass within their start positions for a game of netball (see figure 3.8). Make this a competitive activity with teams trying to finish before other teams.

You could rotate positions or even introduce handicap starts if one team easily outperforms the other. Note that the point of the game is not so much the relay but learning the player positions.

Starting the Game

Following are the three restart options in netball:

- At the start of the game and after a goal has been scored
- When the ball is out and is thrown in
- After a simultaneous infringement that requires a throw-up ball

Fastest Hands (Simultaneous Infringement)

This is a simple activity that can be used as a fun warm-up. However, the point is for players to learn rule infringements in netball and this 'game' is the restart procedure following a simultaneous infringement in netball. The rule relates to the umpire deciding that there has been a simultaneous breach of the rules. Because the umpire is unable to award a penalty pass to one team, this throw-up ball gives both players an opportunity to win the ball and possession for their team (this is the equivalent to a jump ball in basketball).

Two players stand approximately 1.5 metres apart with their hands at their sides. The third player holds a netball just above waist height between the two players. The third player, also acting as the umpire, calls 'Play' and releases the ball. The other two players snatch at the ball as fast as they can. The winner is the player who gets the ball. You can have them play best of three restarts and rotate the three players.

In this activity, the only tactic is anticipating the umpire's call.

Pass-In and Goal Shooting

A restart in netball after the ball has gone out of play requires the player to place one foot close to the boundary line before throwing the ball into play. Players need to know that they cannot pass the ball over two thirds of the court. This restart activity starts with an uncontested throw-in and a 2v1 playing situation to practise goal shooting.

Set up the practice as in figure 3.9a. There are four players: A goal attack (GA), who inbounds the ball; a wing defence (WD), who receives the inbound pass in the centre third and returns it to the goal attack (GA); a goal shooter (GS), who works with the goal attack (GA) to score a goal; and a goalkeeper

(GK), who defends against the attackers. Players rotate as per figure 3.9b.

A quick interchange pass between the goal attack and wing defence starts the play. The goal attack and goal shooter try to score a goal against the goalkeeper. The play lasts until a goal is scored or the two attackers infringe the rules or turn the ball over. At that point, players rotate their positions. It is important that this activity be refereed.

This activity is designed to reinforce the restart rules of the pass-in. To give it direction, a 2v1 goal-shooting activity is included to allow players to practise goal shooting in an open-skill environment.

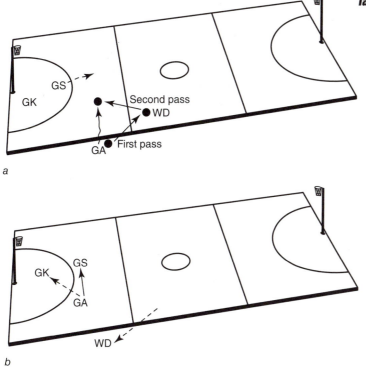

a

b

FIGURE 3.9 Restart practice set-up (*a*) and rotation (*b*).

Tactics

- **Goalkeeper (GK):** The 2v1 practice should make it very difficult for the goalkeeper to stop a shot at goal. However, by employing man-to-man marking, the goalkeeper can put pressure on the passer to anticipate the goal shooter's move to receive the ball. Inside the goal-shooting circle, he can defend the shot and try to collect the rebound if the shot misses.

- **Goal shooter (GS) and goal attack (GA):** After the goal attack inbounds the ball, they should dodge close to the goal-scoring circle to receive the return pass. The goal shooter may have to make several quick dodges into space to receive a pass. The two players should inter-pass until one player feels comfortable about taking the shot at goal.

Pass-Off

● ●

▶ Equipment

- One netball per game
- Netball bibs to distinguish player positions and roles

▶ Formation

There are four attackers (wing defence, centre, goal attack and wing attack) and three on-court defenders (centre, wing defence and goal defence). Set up the game as in figure 3.10. The fourth player for the defensive team acts as umpire.

▶ Recipe

Explain the basic starting procedure. The objects of the game are to learn how to start the game of netball or to restart it after a goal has been scored, and to try to score a goal. In this game, a goal is worth 1 point. Also, in this game, only the goal attack can score a goal, and she can only be defended in the goal circle by the goal defence.

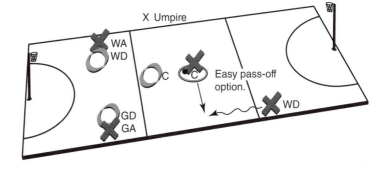

FIGURE 3.10 Setup for Pass-Off.

The fourth defensive player, who is off the court, starts the game by calling 'Play'. She also records the score. Rotate this function among the defensive team players.

Each group of four has five attacks to achieve a maximum possible score of 5 points.

The attack restarts if a goal is scored or the defenders force a turnover. After five attacks, teams reverse roles. To maintain interest and learning, either have players rotate their positions while playing the same team, or play another team.

▶ Rules

Netball rules apply. If infringements or simultaneous infringements occur, or if the ball goes out from a defender, apply the rules and restart the game to teach the rules. If the attackers infringe or lose the ball, the attack is finished.

▶ Tactics

- **Attackers:** The easy pass-off option is the pass back to the wing defence. Attackers should establish a pattern by using that pass and then suddenly change to find a more direct pass-off option. The wing defence should not be neglected in general play and should be used for a back pass if attackers are all marked. In this way, the attacking team can make use of its numerical playing advantage.

- **Defenders:** Starting with the centre, defenders need to concentrate on marking the receivers. Because the attacking wing defence cannot score, marking that player is sometimes a misuse of resources. Defenders need to man-to-man mark the other players, and when the attackers move, try to anticipate their movements.

● ●

Conclusion

Novice players will need a little time to pick up on all the rules and procedures of netball. However, the game approach should provide a relatively straightforward but enjoyable context within which to learn the rules and restart procedures of the game. After all, they do want to play netball.

4

Applying TGfU to Teaching Football

Football, soccer, the beautiful game—call it what you will, it is the biggest participant sport in the world. Even in my own rugby-obsessed country (New Zealand) there are more junior (under 13 years) registered soccer than rugby players (Sport and Recreation New Zealand, SPARC, 2006). However, despite the game's worldwide popularity, it was my teaching experience in physical education classes that the game was played so appallingly by my New Zealand students that it bore little resemblance to the fast-paced passing game that captivates audiences worldwide. Wanting my novices to the game to experience the feel of a game that is associated with completing successive passes, running fast and dodging opponents, but seeing that they were unable to even control the direction of a kicked ball, provided the motivation to find another way to teach this wonderful game to novice players.

In a minor piece of research (Slade, 2003), I introduced undergraduate physical education teacher trainees to various motor skill instructional methods. In turn, they instructed sixty students ages 11 to 13, divided into groups of ten, the game of football using either a traditional skills-based approach, a group-based mastery learning method or a TGfU method. Two of the several measures of the effectiveness of the methodologies employed in the project were to be the number of shots on goal the randomly assigned teams made in an end-of-programme tournament, and which team won the tournament.

The teams that made the most shots on goal were those taught using the group-based mastery methodology. However, the teams that actually won the most games were those that received the TGfU instruction. The difference among the teams was not so much in technique but in the distribution and positioning of the players and their understanding of the various roles within the game.

The TGfU-instructed teams only marginally missed out on having the most shots on goal. However, seemingly as a result of their understanding of the principles of attack and defence, they frequently outnumbered their opponents' defenders, which led to more of their shots on goal being successful. Interestingly, they conceded fewer goals than the other teams did, and opposition attackers seldom outnumbered their defenders.

Football players can have more success—and fun—by improving their skill and knowledge.

101

This chapter uses the TGfU model used in that small project to introduce football to students who are novices to the game. My experience has been that the format works best in coeducational physical education classes of mixed ability, although I have used aspects of this approach quite successfully in my own coaching of football teams. The sequence and structure of the games allows for both the performance of the movement skills of the games and the development of declarative knowledge relative to rules and tactics. The games used in this section also expose obvious technique deficiencies. If you do not have extensive content knowledge to deal with teaching the techniques of this game, help is not far away. There are libraries full of how-to-play-football manuals, DVDs and videos.

I have included only one or two specific assessment activities in this introduction to football. However, because players need feedback and assessment on their development, I recommend that you read chapter 5 on assessment in conjunction with this unit of work as the assessment procedures discussed in chapter 5 are easily applied to football.

The basic strategy of the game of football is simple: Players attempt to score a goal by putting the ball into their opponents' goal. Field players attempt to do this either by kicking or heading the ball. As the saying goes, easier said than done!

LEARNING SEQUENCE

The first highly modified game has as its focus movement with and without the ball, keeping possession, understanding defensive principles and back and around passes. Players are then introduced in sequence to trapping the ball, using the throw-in as a restart from the side of the playing area, the basic side-foot pass, dribbling the ball and zone defence. Tackling and heading are not taught in this sequence but would logically be the next techniques of the game to learn.

Note that I supply only a sequence of learning and not specific lessons. You need to decide how much time you want to spend on, and what content you want to include in, each lesson. The lesson sequence may take you 5 or 10 lessons to complete. Base your decisions on what you do on the characteristics of your class.

FLICK UP, CATCH AND RUN

In this skill practice players learn the following fundamental movements:

- Rolling a ball
- Flicking up a ball and catching it
- Running and dodging

Align the players in pairs about 5 to 7 metres (about 6 to 8 yd) apart with a ball. Demonstrate how to roll the ball accurately along the ground to a partner. Next, teach the players that by pointing their toes at the ball and allowing the rolled ball to roll up their foot, they can, with a small flick of the foot, lift the ball off the ground without using their hands and then catch it.

Explain that in the game they are about to play the ball will be rolled to them along the ground and they can either trap the ball football style with their feet or flick it up and catch it. Once they have the ball, they can run with it. The flick-up skill results in very fast continuous movements. Explain that they cannot stop the ball with their hands.

Continue the 'Flick-up' practice activity for 1 or 2 minutes encouraging the players once they have caught the ball to run 3 to 5 metres before returning the ball to their partner. Note this sequence breaks with the TGfU model of always starting with a game. You could go straight to the game if your sole aim was to preserve the integrity of the TGfU model but my experience is that the two to three minutes of practice of this technique results in a much better game.

Flick-Ball

● ●

▸**Learning Objectives**

Players will learn declarative tactical knowledge associated with the following:

- Basic rules of starting and restarts in football
- Tactics associated with keeping the ball including back and around passes

- Importance of marking particular areas of the field
- Movement off the ball

▸**Equipment**

- One football per 10 to 12 players
- 10 cones
- Bibs to distinguish teams

Formation

Two teams of five or six players oppose each other on a playing area approximately 50 by 20 metres (about 55 by 22 yd). Each team starts inside its own defensive half. Once the game starts, there is no offside.

Recipe

Players attempt to score goals by running or rolling the ball, always to a team-mate, anywhere over the end line. If they succeed in this, they receive 1 point. In the middle of the goal line is a goal. If they either run the ball through the goal or pass (i.e., roll) it through the goal to a member of their team who legitimately stops the ball with her feet, this goal is worth 5 points.

The ball must not be thrown but must be rolled along the ground. When a player is attempting to score a goal by passing it over the goal line, the goal only counts if a team-mate stops the ball with her feet.

Players may stop the ball with their feet, pick it up and run with it. They may also employ the previously learned skill of flicking the ball up and then running with it. The flick-up greatly increases the speed of the game. Once in possession of the ball, a player may then move the ball by rolling it to a partner or by running with it. The team without the ball tries to intercept passes or force turnovers. Tagging the player with the ball constitutes a tackle. If tagged, the player must stop and attempt to pass the ball. Because there is no limit to the number of tackles a team may have, they can retain possession for quite a lengthy period of time as is seen by elite level teams. Defending players must stand one or two steps away from a tackled player to allow her to make a pass. A player may not pass the ball to herself.

A ball out of play is rolled in to restart the game. A restart after the ball has gone over the goal line by the attackers but is not a goal is taken from the middle of the playing area in front of the 5-point goal. It is roll passed to restart the game in the manner of a football goal kick. A restart after a defending team has put the ball out over its own defensive goal line is taken by the attacking team by rolling the ball into play from the corner flag or cone closest to the side where the ball went out. This restart in football from a corner of the field is called a corner

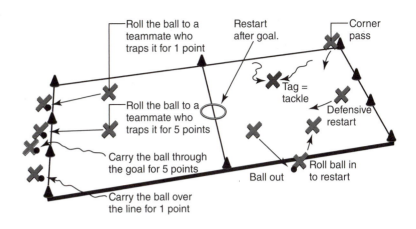

FIGURE 4.1 Scoring options for Flick-Ball.

kick. Restarting after a goal requires all players to be in their own defensive halves. The pass-off must go forward before it is passed back.

In this game there is no goalie in the traditional football sense of the game. That means that a player is not assigned to be the goalie and therefore no one may stop shots at goal with her hands. All players in this game are field players.

Rules

- Each team has the same number of players.

- The ball can only be stopped or flicked up with the feet (i.e., players may not use their hands). Once she has stopped the ball, a player may pick it up and run with it or pass it. The only way to pass the ball is to roll it. Players may pass the ball while running with it.

- A tackle is made by tagging the player with the ball. A tackled player must stop, retreat to the point where she was tagged and pass the ball. There are no limits to the number of tackles teams may incur.

- Defenders must stand at least two steps away from a tackled player to allow her to make a pass.

- To restart the game if the ball goes out over the sideline, the team that did not put the ball out rolls it in.

- No offside. There is no offside in this game except at the start of a game or after a goal is scored. Play is started or restarted at halfway with all players in their defensive half.

- Restarts after the ball has gone over the opposition goal line but has not scored a goal are made by a player rolling the ball from the area in front of the 5-point goal area

- Goals are scored in two ways:

  1. A player runs the ball over the goal line (1 point) or through the centre goal (5 points) without being tagged.

  2. A ball is passed and trapped over the goal line (1 point) or through the centre goal (5 points). A 'passed' goal is only scored if the ball is trapped by a team-mate over the end line.

- After a goal is scored, all players must retreat to their own defensive halves. The game is restarted by a pass from the centre of the playing area at the halfway point. The pass-off must go forward but can then be passed back. Players may not pass the ball to themselves.

- To ensure safety, pushing and leg tripping are not allowed.

- There are no designated goalies in this game.

▶ Tactics and Strategies

The major strategic focus of this game is keeping possession of the ball. Typically, this is extremely difficult for novice footballers. However, rolling the ball results in accurate passes and makes this a realistic outcome even with novices. The no-offside rule and mandating that a ball passed over the goal line counts as a goal only if it is trapped by a team-mate also force the players to play in front of the ball and move into space off the ball.

Your experience of many of the other games in this text should prepare you well for commenting on tactics required for this game. However, first let the players become familiar with the game with little interference. Letting the game unfold and encouraging the players to use the flick-up when receiving the ball fulfills another major outcome of this introduction to football, namely to allow novice players to experience football as a fast, running, dodging, passing game.

▶ Variations

This requires the addition of an attacking zone 10 metres (about 11 yd) out from each goal line that crosses the width of the field (reread the Pass Back variation of Piltz Pass in chapter 1, on page 37, to see how this concept will work in this game).

Following are rule modifications using the Piltz Pass variation applied to this game:

- If a player is tagged with the ball outside of the attacking zone, her first pass must be lateral or backwards towards her defensive goal.

- If a player passes forward after being tagged outside of the attacking quarter, a turnover is awarded to the opposition.

- If a player is tagged in the attacking zone, she may still make a forward pass.

There are several tactical objectives behind these rule changes. First, players learn the back and around passing concept, in which a team keeps possession by passing the ball backwards to an area less congested by opponents, who typically are trying to get in front of the attackers to defend their goal.

A second reason for the rule changes is to teach on-ball attacking support play. If at least one player does not support, from behind, the on-ball attacker and that attacker is tagged while in possession of the ball, then a forward attacker has to run back to receive the next pass. This slows down the attack, and such receivers are easily seen and marked. Having a support player already in position allows the player in possession to make the back pass quickly. Also, the back pass can change the point of attack, especially if it is also a lateral pass.

Third, the application of the Pass Back rules from Piltz Pass is designed to encourage the player with the ball to pass before she is tagged. Passing before she is tagged, or tackled, gives her a forward pass option and discourages her from running with the ball when a pass is on. It also contributes to a feeling that the game has momentum.

Yet a further outcome of the application of the Piltz Pass, Pass Back rule is that it allows players to see more clearly the concept of offensive depth. While the attackers are passing the ball back or laterally, they are still attacking, but these attacks are launched from a deeper defensive position than players normally associate with the concept of attacking in games. The back pass ensures that all players have to spread out more over the length of the playing area, creating longitudinal space referred to as offensive depth.

Continuing to allow the forward pass in the attacking quarter is important because you do not want to teach a holding or defensive ploy in an area where players should be encouraged to take risks.

Questions that should be directed to students about these concepts can be found in the Piltz Pass game (page 38).

Questions

Q: How do players restart the game after a goal?

A: All players must return to their half of the field and the team just scored against restarts the game with a pass that must first travel forward.

Q: How is the game restarted after a defender puts the ball out over her own goal line?

A: A pass is taken from the corner of the field on the side of the goal where the ball went out by the attacking team. In football it is called a corner.

Q: How are goals scored?

A: Running or passing the ball over the goal line. A ball passed over the back line must be trapped to count as a goal.

Q: Why are centre goals worth 5 points?

A: Because the centre goal is easier to defend than the whole back line, these goals are more difficult to score. In addition, the extra points help focus the players to that part of the field where in authentic football the goal is situated.

Q: What would be the main priority for a defender left by herself to defend an attack she cannot stop?

A: Not to defend the 1-point goal but prevent a 5-point goal

Q: When one's team has the ball on attack, what is the tactical advantage of spreading the team out?

A: It forces the defenders to spread out to mark your team and this creates more space in which to play.

TRAPPING

While continuing to develop the players' understanding of the basic restart rules found in football, the major point of the modified version of the previous game is to introduce the technique of trapping the ball within the context of the game. This new game is called Trap-Ball.

Before playing Trap-Ball, players need to be introduced to the basic skill of trapping a football.

Two players stand 5 to 7 metres (about 6 to 8 yd) apart, and one player has the ball. Demonstrate two basic trapping techniques to the players—the side-foot trap and the heel trap, in which the foot is placed on the ball, heel down, to jam the ball between the foot and the ground (see figure 4.2).

Once they have seen the demonstration, players roll the ball to each other, trapping it, picking it up and then rolling it back to their partners. This should continue for 1 or 2 minutes until you are satisfied that the players understand the basic idea of the technique. Because rolling is the passing method

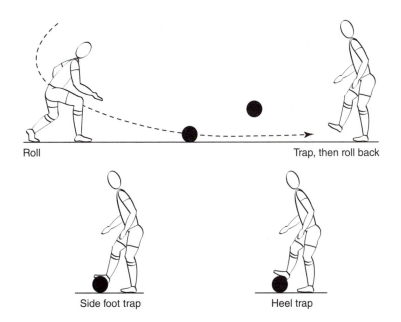

Roll   Trap, then roll back

Side foot trap   Heel trap

FIGURE 4.2 Trapping technique.

used in Trap-Ball, this practice session helps players deliver accurate passes that their partners can trap. Once the technique is mastered to a rudimentary level, play Trap-Ball.

Trap-Ball

The only difference between this game and Flick-Ball is that players are now *not* allowed to flick the ball up. Players must trap the ball before they can pick it up and either run with it or pass it. This will teach them how to trap the ball within the context of a game. The roll pass will improve the chances of the players receiving accurate passes within the game so they can practise the trap.

Provide feedback on trapping technique either informally or through authentic assessment opportunities (see chapter 5). Also, continue to keep the main focus on the tactics of the game (i.e., moving into space, having players both in front and behind the ball carrier and finding space by passing the ball back towards their own goal).

Note: Teams still do not play with goalies, so no one, even when defending a shot for a goal, may stop the ball with their hands.

Ask your players the following questions:

Q: When trapping the ball, should the foot move towards the ball or give slightly on contact?

A: Give slightly to absorb the pace of the ball.

Q: What is the tactical advantage of having team-mates in front of and behind the ball carrier?

A: It provides both forward and back passing options forcing opponents to spread out in defence, thus giving more space in which your team-mates may receive the ball.

Q: What is the tactical advantage of always having one player standing deep behind the team when the team is in possession of the ball?

A: It always gives a safe outlet possession pass; it provides a good place for someone to see all of the game and provide feedback to the forward players, and it also ensures the team has a defensive player ready to stop any counter-attacks.

TRAP AND THROW-IN

Players will obviously know that in football one does not pick up the ball and run with it or roll it as a pass. However, explain that the point of slowly moving to the authentic game in this fashion is to ensure that even as novices they actually get to feel the game a little bit like elite players do, especially in terms of the pace of the game and successfully completing passes.

In progressing to the authentic game, the next technique to be learned is the throw-in and trap.

Football is an unusual game in that, although the game is essentially about controlling the ball with the feet, when the ball goes out, it is thrown in. Performing the throw-in is relatively straightforward, but controlling the bouncing ball is quite difficult. So, before moving to the throw-in, teach how to trap a ball that bounces just in front of the player.

Set players up on a grid with one ball for every two or three players. Demonstrate a basic side-foot and heel trap of a lobbed ball. Explain that it is important to give each partner the best chance of trapping the ball, so they must do their best to lob pass accurately.

Skill 1: Players lob the ball to each other, trying to make it bounce immediately in front of their partner so they can easily practise the trap technique (see figure 4.3). Players trap

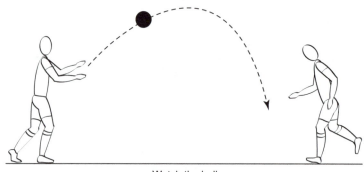

Watch the ball
Adjust position—move to trap the ball
Don't let the ball bounce—squeeze it against the ground

FIGURE 4.3 Technique for trapping a ball bounced just in front of a player.

the ball, pick it up and lob the ball back for their partner to trap.

Skill 2: Demonstrate the throw-in technique (see figure 4.4a-b) and the associated rules both in the release of the ball and the offside rule. In twos or threes, players practise the throw-in across the 7 metres (about 8 yd) of the grid.

a   Ball behind head, use two hands, and keep feet on ground

b   Upper body forward
Arms follow through on release
Feet on ground

FIGURE 4.4   Technique for the throw-in.

Throw and Trap Practice

▶Learning Objectives

Players will do the following:

- Throw the ball in correctly
- Recognise when the thrower is ready to throw and the receiver is ready to receive a throw-in
- Move into space to receive the throw
- Throw the ball over varying distances

▶Equipment

One ball among three players

▶Formation

Choose a playing area that is about 14 by 21 metres (about 15 by 23 yd; see grid layout in the introduction). One player is positioned on the outside of the playing area while the other stands inside of the playing area. The third player (feedback assessor) observes the game and marks the feedback sheet.

▶Recipe

Receivers move about inside the designated area looking to find space and using basic communication (calling or body language) to receive a throw-in from their partner. Players cannot receive consecutive throws in the same place. After trapping the ball, players return the ball to the thrower. Each player receives 10 throw-ins before rotating roles with his partner (figure 4.5).

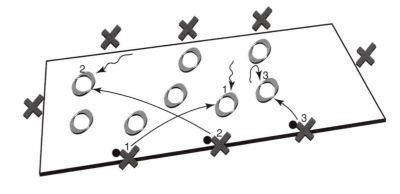

FIGURE 4.5   Practicing throwing and trapping.

The player in the role of feedback assessor is able to provide constructive feedback for the other players while also developing his own knowledge of the skill. The form below shows a sample assessment form that could be used. The judgments, based on the criteria provided, are very simple for the assessor to interpret and mark, but they provide good feedback for the person throwing the ball in and the receiver.

Game: Trap and Throw-In   **Trapper:** Sally

Number of throws received	Missed the ball	Three touches of the ball	Two touches of the ball	One touch of the ball
Totals	2	4	3	1

Comments:

The first couple of throws you completely missed the ball. On the throws where you took three touches, you semed to kick the ball, but by the end of the throws you were much softer with your feet and started to make really good traps.

Game: More Trap-Ball   **Thrower:** Mary

Number of throws	Legitimate throws	Illegitimate (foul) throws	Timing and distance of throw: improvement needed	Timing and distance of throw: good
Totals	9	1	2	8

Comments:

The first throw was not far enough behind your head, so it was a foul throw. All of the other throws were fine.

You and Sally did not coordinate too well on the first two throws. On the following throws, though, the timing and body language between you and Sally was excellent. These throws were all on target to give her a good chance of making a trap.

More Trap-Ball

In this game, players continue to play Trap-Ball, further developing their understanding of the tactical and movement fundamentals of the previous games, but the adaption to the previous version of this game is that now, when the ball goes out over the sideline, it has to be thrown in. It is important to referee the rules governing the throw-in to assist the players with their understanding of what is and is not allowed during this game restart.

▸ Variations

A team throwing the ball in has the option of calling 'Safety'. A 'safety' call requires that the ball be thrown back towards the team's own goal, but the throw-in is not contestable by the opposition. That is, the ball is thrown in to a nominated player who is allowed to trap it and pick it up without the opposition being allowed to take the ball from him. However, after picking up the ball, the player must make a pass; he may not run with the ball. Once he makes the pass, the game continues as previously.

▸ Questions

Q: What are the rules of the throw-in in football in relation to hands on the ball, feet on the ground and ball behind the head?

A: Both hands must be on the ball and the ball must be taken behind and then delivered over the thrower's head. Both feet need to be on the ground and outside of the field of play when the ball is released.

Q: In football can a player be offside at a throw-in?

A: No.

Q: What methods of communication, other than calling for the ball, should the receiver use to tell the player throwing the ball in that she is ready to receive it?

A: Facial expressions, eye contact, hand directions.

Q: What is the tactical advantage of the receiver of a throw-in immediately playing the ball back to the person who threw it to him?

A: The person who just threw the ball in is almost always left unmarked.

SIDE-FOOT PASS

The next technique to be introduced to the game is the push, or side-foot, pass. Many football coaches explain this passing action as knocking the ball ('Knock it!'). In pairs, players will learn the following in relation to the side foot pass:

- Body position
- Foot action
- Follow-through and recovery

The side-foot pass is delivered over distances up to 15 metres (about 16 yd), although the composition of your class should determine the practice distance. For novices, the 7-metre (8 yd) grids (see page xvi) are ideal dimensions for practicing this technique. The ball is played along the ground directly to the feet of a team-mate.

The non-striking foot is placed beside the ball in a comfortable position to support the player. The head is almost over the top of the ball, and the weight is transferred forward. The leg action consists of a short back lift from the striking leg, bending at the knee (see figure 4.6a). The upper leg swings through, and the lower leg snaps forward with the foot turned out to provide the wide area of the foot arch as the contact area against the ball. After striking the ball, the player follows through with a short, jabbing-type action (see figure 4.6b).

The player places the ball and, using a one- or three-step approach, passes the ball to a partner. The partner traps and returns the ball. Have players practise over various distances. Look for a smooth action and good timing. Common faults are having the head up and not over the ball. Keep the distances short so players don't feel they need to generate a lot of power in the shot.

a   Head over ball
Striking leg bent at knee
Foot beside ball, turned out

b

FIGURE 4.6 Side-foot pass technique.

Knock It!

In this activity, students continue to work on all of the outcomes of the previous games in this sequence, as well as on using the side-foot pass within a game context. The same equipment and game formations are needed as in the previous game.

There are two rule changes in this activity to bring to the attention of the players. First, after trapping the ball, players have the option of using the side-foot kick to pass the ball. However, do not allow players to 'first-time' kick the ball. They must make an effort to trap the ball. If they trap the ball and are then tagged, they still have the option of either picking up the ball and making a rolled pass or using the new skill of the side-foot pass.

The first-time pass is the ultimate aim of passing in the game of football, but at the novice stage such attempts are extremely haphazard in terms of accuracy. Allowing the first-time pass at this stage with novices encourages an uncontrolled swing at the ball without any thought given to where the ball might end up. Insisting on a trap also reinforces the continued development of that technique in a game context.

The second rule change in this activity from the previous games is that in addition to the previous methods of scoring, rolling or running the ball over the end line or through the goal, goals may now also be scored by passing the ball over the goal line using the side-foot kick pass. Note that, to count as a goal, the ball, even when passed with the foot, needs to be trapped over the goal line by one of the passer's team-mates.

It is not compulsory to use the side-foot pass in this game. Because it is paramount to keep the pace in the game, encourage players to pick up the ball and run with it or roll pass the ball if they wish to. However, to move the players ever closer to the authentic game, point out how much quicker it is to trap and side-foot pass the ball than it is to trap it, pick it up and roll it. To encourage the development of the trap and side-foot pass, provide positive feedback when you see players using this technique.

In addition do not be afraid of coming back to and repeating the side-foot practice in the grids. However, keep those practices brief and return to the game so players can practise the skill within the context of the game.

▶ Variations

If players choose to pick up the ball and run with it, make it a rule that they may only use the roll pass while they are moving. If they are tagged, they must stop and use the side-foot pass. At this stage of the player's development, the roll pass is probably faster and more accurate than his use of the side-foot pass, but increasingly you want to lead your students towards the authentic version of the game of football.

DRIBBLING

Before embarking on the next game in the teaching sequence, you need to first teach the fundamentals of the football dribble. In relation to the dribble, players will learn the following:

- Body position
- Foot action

To practise dribbling, players assemble in threes. Two players are on one side of the grid with the ball, and one player is on the other side without a ball. In a continuous relay of threes, the player with the ball dribbles across the grid to the player without the ball. That player then dribbles the ball back across the grid to the next waiting player. In this way the practice dribble 'relay' continues (see figure 4.7). By using the grid system (shown in the introduction) players can dribble the ball over 21 metres (about 23 yd), but you can easily manipulate the style of dribble by regulating the number of touches in each grid.

For example, if you want your players to practise a close, controlled dribble, you might require three or four touches of the ball in each grid. A slightly faster dribble might require only two touches per grid. Finally, require only one touch per grid for a dribble at full speed.

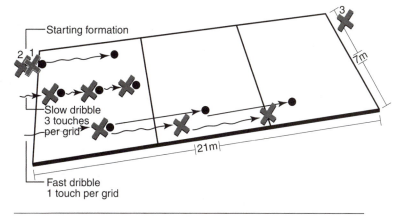

FIGURE 4.7 Dribble practise.

Dribble Game

Having started the chapter with a game that did not involve kicking the ball (a skill extremely fundamental to the game of football), we now arrive at a game in which players can employ the authentic techniques of the game. In this game, players now have the option of dribbling the ball. However, to ensure that the game retains many of the components associated with passing accuracy, and to accommodate the wide discrepancy of ability found in physical education classes, players are still permitted to trap the ball, pick it up and run with it. Also permitted is the roll pass, but I would restrict the use of the roll pass to only being allowed while the player is moving with the ball. Following tags, or tackles, all players must side-foot pass the ball.

This modified game features the following five additions to the rules of the previous games:

- After being tagged, or tackled, players must side-foot kick the ball.

- Players may dribble the ball. Turnovers from dribbling occur if the player loses close control of the ball and another player traps it.

- If a player is dribbling the ball with their foot constantly in contact with the ball, tagging that player is still a tackle. The tagged player keeps possession of the ball but must stop and make a pass.

- All passes following tackles must be kicked.

- Dribbling the ball over the goal line or through the centre goal is now another method to score goals.

Note: After trapping the ball, a player may still choose to pick up the ball and run with it. This ensures that the players decide their progression into the authentic game; those who are struggling with the skill of dribbling the ball football style, by picking up the ball, can still contribute to their team's performance in the manner of a fast-paced game.

Using the tag as tackle when a player is allowed to dribble the ball can make calling it difficult for the umpire. To simplify the issue, award a turnover to an opponent who can trap a ball that is away from the foot of the player who is dribbling. If the player has close contact with the ball, a tag is a tackle and does not result in a turnover. The tagged player has to stop and pass the ball.

Reinforce all of the other outcomes from the previous games, especially those related to finding space and keeping possession of the ball. Provide plenty of positive reinforcement for students trying to use the trapping, side-foot passing and dribbling skills.

Modified Zone Defence

The objective of this game is to apply an adapted version of the game Zone Defence (in chapter 2) to the sport of football. Players need to see the connection between this game and the need to mark space in front of their goal.

This version of Zone Defence has been modified to reflect the difficulty novices have controlling a football especially in terms of making accurate passes. The main modification is to give the attacking team a force ratio advantage of 6v3 field defenders and a goalie.

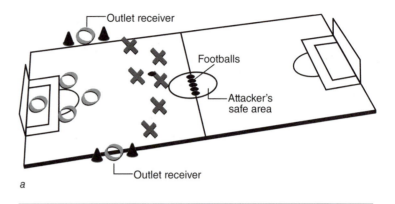

FIGURE 4.8   Setup for Modified Zone Defence.

▶ Learning Objectives

Players will do the following:

- Learn how a zone defence is applied to football
- Use teamwork on both attack and defence

▶ Equipment per Twelve Players

- A soccer or similar goal
- Four small cones
- Five footballs
- Bibs to distinguish teams

▶ Formation

Set out the game as per figure 4.8 and create two teams of six players. The defensive team has one player as their goalkeeper, three field player defenders and two receivers in the pass-out clearing area. The two pass-out options are the clearance areas the defence tries to get the ball to after a turnover. If they clear to one of the two areas on the side of the playing area, they receive defensive points. The attacking team has five attacks to try and score five goals. There is no offside rule in this game.

▶ Recipe

Starting with five balls at the end of the playing area and using the football skills of passing, trapping and dribbling (picking up the ball and running with it is not allowed), the attacking team has five attacks to try and score five goals. All the rules of authentic football apply. A ball out by a defender is thrown in. Defenders putting the ball over their goal line is a corner kick for the attackers. However, if the

attackers put the ball out that attack is finished. The attacking team also has a safety area at the back of the playing area into which the opposition players cannot go. Attackers can back pass the ball into this area and have 10 seconds to restart their attack. A goal is worth two points. The defending team may change the player roles after each attack has been completed.

An attack is over under any of the following conditions:

- A goal is scored (2 points).
- The attackers lose control and put the ball out of bounds. (Out of bounds by the defenders results in a restart and the attack continues.)
- The defenders intercept the ball and pass it to one of their receivers waiting between the cones placed on the side of the playing area. A successful pass to a receiver by a defender is worth one point

Allowing the defenders to score points encourages them to do more than just kick the ball away when they get possession. It also teaches the attackers to immediately switch from attack to defence if their team loses the ball. After five attacks the teams change roles.

Note: If the ball is lost or put out over the sideline or goal line by an attacker but no goal is scored, that attack is completed and the attackers get another ball and start the next attack. Attackers can score a maximum of 10 points. Defenders can score a maximum of 5 points. The final score is the team's combined scores from both attacking and defending.

▶ Tactics and Strategies

The numerical advantage for the attackers can be exploited only if they spread out and pass the ball accurately to their teammates. They could look to use 2v1 attacking scenarios to beat defenders or pass the ball around to find an unmarked player who has a chance to shoot for goal. If they lose the ball, they must quickly block off the outlet passes available to the defenders in order to regain possession and to stop them scoring defensive points

The numerical advantage also means that the defenders cannot man-to-man defend, so they need to adopt a zone defence to protect their goal. If they get possession of the ball, they must try and pass the ball to one of their receivers waiting on the side of the field between the cones. In this game, apart from saving goals, the goalkeeper has an important role in talking to the defenders and keeping their defence well coordinated.

▶ Questions

Attackers

Q: Why is it important to pass quickly to team-mates?

A: Quick passes force the defenders to keep adjusting their positions. This can lead to confusion in the defence and easy chances for the attackers to score goals.

Q: If the defenders are well set up in defence, what are the attackers' best options?

A: To position themselves so they can pass both across and behind the defenders to force them to constantly adjust their defensive positions. They should be patient and even take the ball back to the safe zone and start the attack again.

Q:: If the ball is intercepted by the defenders, what must the attackers do immediately?

A: Defend against the outlet passes the defenders will be trying to achieve, regain the ball and continue their attack.

Defenders

Q: If the attackers pass the ball around (e.g., from left to right) and attack from the other side, how should the defenders move to stop their attack?

A: They should slide from left to right with the attack.

Q: Is talking in defence important? Why?

A: Yes. In many games defenders cannot see all of the attackers, and they need advice on where to move to ensure that all attackers are being marked. In this game, the goalie is best positioned to do most of the talking on defence.

· ·

CONCLUSION

An aim of the teaching approach presented in this chapter is to give novices the chance to experience the speed of football and what it feels like to maintain possession of the ball that is so important to the enjoyment of football but typically enjoyed only by elite players. Another primary aim is to provide a structure that takes into account the discrepancy in ability, often found in physical education classes, between those students with extensive backgrounds in sport and those who are novices. Students at both ends of the ability continuum can play alongside each other and enjoy this game. In these games, the novice is able to contribute and feel part of the positive social experience that can result from playing a team game.

Note these games are designed only as an introduction to football. However, even for experienced players games such as Flick-Ball and Modified Zone Defence can be a lot of fun and used to reinforce basic football strategies.

5

Authentic Assessment

'Well played, Caroline. Your pass completion rate has gone from 30 to 75 percent! Your decision making, especially your goal to make the early easy pass rather than dribble, is paying dividends. In your last drive to the basket, the opponents were so used to you passing that they gave you an easy layup.'

'Okay, Luke, as team statistician, is there anything about your team's cooperative play that could explain your improved defensive record?'

'Well, everyone's off-ball defensive support play has really improved. Richard and Andrew are working at 100 percent, but more importantly, I can report that after a turnover of possession, the team's average off-ball defensive support play is now up to 90 percent from our previous 60 percent. I think that explains a lot!'

Assessment in the form of feedback like the preceding does not require expensive equipment; nor does it come at the expense of fun or playing a game. In fact, it depends on game play. Your players engage in cooperative player behaviour and set individual goals while you provide authentic and extremely valuable feedback on their understanding of games. Authentic assessment requires that you be familiar with basic game outcomes, tactics or techniques, but it does not require that you be an expert.

The type of assessment illustrated in this chapter also provides opportunites for you to provide team feedback rather than always giving individual feedback. Of course a team is the sum of the whole, but we often overlook the team cooperative function. Sometimes improving performance in team games is not about technique but about the team playing cooperatively, being supportive of team-mates and socialising together.

Authentic assessment can also provide opportunities to develop in context associated aspects of games, for example, leadership or communication skills. These qualities are often claimed as learning outcomes associated with playing games, but unfortunately they are often not taught. Consequently if the qualities do emerge, it is more the result of luck than directed learning experiences. A game umpiring scenario is provided in this chapter to illustrate an authentic context in which to observe a player's developing confidence and ability to speak and communicate in front of her peers.

Authentic assessment can enhance cooperative team play.
© Gary John Norman/Stone/Getty Images

This chapter demonstrates how authentic assessment can be integrated into game sessions so that it does not disturb—but rather, enhances—both game sense and the playing experience.

ENHANCING LEARNING AND GAME PERFORMANCE

TGfU gives you tremendous scope in which to undertake authentic game assessments. Authentic assessment integrated into the teaching programme enhances learning by providing students not only with feedback on their learning but also a whole new perspective on team games. The following comments are what I frequently hear from physical education teachers when the topic of practical or game assessment is raised.

'I don't have time for assessment. By the time I've taught them the skills, rules and how to play the game, there just isn't time for testing their skills.'

'The students don't want to waste time doing assessments when they could be playing the game. They resent it, become bored and are quickly off task.'

'I've got a choice: Either teach them the skills or do assessment. I know what is really useful so I avoid all skill assessment.'

These comments reflect a perspective of assessment that is summative, usually about specific technique performance, takes place in stand-alone lessons and does not enhance the learning of the game or sport.

Assessment as addressed in this chapter is not about collecting data to provide a grade. Rather, it is about enhancing students' understanding of, and performance in, games. Authentic assessment also provides feedback on the effectiveness of your instruction. Of course, the assessment procedures suggested in this chapter could be used as a basis for report writing, but that is not the main intent. When both assessing and being assessed, students should gain insights into game play in a manner that contributes to their own and the team's performance as well as their appreciation of games and sports from an observer's perspective.

WHAT IS AUTHENTIC ASSESSMENT?

Authentic game assessment relates to how the game is played. As much as possible it relates to

and describes what takes place or what players or even officials do within the game. For example, an authentic assessment of the football side-foot pass might involve counting the number of attempts a player made to use that type of pass within a set period of time within the game. An even more important assessment could be the number of times the pass reached its intended target (sometimes called pass completions).

By contrast, a traditional skills-based assessment of the use of the side-foot pass used in football might consist of how many such passes two players make from stationary positions 7 metres (about 8 yd) apart in 1 minute. This traditional line passing assessment provides unrealistic data. The performance context is closed skill, with little or no decision making required. Certainly there is no pressure in terms of consequences of a poor pass on the passer. The adage 'it takes two to make a pass' is not recognised in this type of assessment.

Using authentic assessment within game-based assessment as in the manner of the just mentioned football side-foot pass gives both teacher and learner feedback on the progress of learning in their use of the side-foot pass within an authentic context. Of course, the example merely scratches the surface of the potential of this assessment. Other variables that could be assessed include technique, decision making, movement off the ball to get into space, calling, use of body language or even levels of fatigue.

The authentic game assessment examples presented in this chapter provide means of gathering and using :

- Data from game contexts to use in discussions with the players or the team
- Player feedback and motivation for further practice to improve game performance
- Feedback on your practice structure and clear indications as to what else you might need to include in your players' practices

ASSESSING DECLARATIVE KNOWLEDGE AND AFFECT

To successfully play a game, there has to be a shared and agreed understanding of the rules. To ensure that understanding exists, one form of game assessment is to evaluate the students' declarative knowledge relating to rules and tactics and affective outcomes. This type of assessment can be used as both a diagnostic and summative tool. You can use it as a diagnostic tool to establish, before instruction, the students' declarative knowledge relative to rules and tactics associated with the game. It can also provide feedback on affective outcomes relative to students' perceived level of anticipated enjoyment or success in the activity. After the activity, repeating the assessment gives you summative feedback on the effectiveness of your instruction at both declarative and affective levels. You can undertake this type of assessment quickly and one or two lessons ahead of the planned instruction dates. The results you receive can help you decide whether you need to modify your intended programme of instruction.

The following sections address areas to include in an authentic assessment. Form 5.1 shows an example of a field hockey assessment that includes these areas. You can easily adapt the questions in this form to the sport or game you intend to cover.

Playing Background

Establishing the students' playing background allows you to reflect on whether your programme of instruction matches the ability level of your students. If you want to organise teams in advance of the lessons, you must decide whether you will have teams of mixed experience levels or graded teams based on students' experience of the game.

Understanding of Basic Rules

Successful and fun game play requires a shared understanding of game rules. The questions in form 5.1 establish what students already know about the basic rules—in this case, rules relating to restarts in field hockey. The feedback from these questions will help you determine what you need to teach so students can play with a shared understanding of the rules. At an introductory field hockey level, for example, players need to know what to do after a ball has gone out of play or a goal has been scored.

A good way to teach rules while also developing players' communication skills is to have students officiate as umpires or referees in games. Before allowing them to do this, you must first teach and reinforce the basic rules within play in quite a deliberate manner. Then, assigning students to the officiating role provides a powerful learning experience to reinforce that knowledge. It also helps reinforce the importance of other aspects of the game experience—namely, that games require officials as an integral part of the wider game, or sport, experience.

With less experienced or shy students, a buddy umpire is an excellent strategy. The buddy, working beside the umpire, quietly makes the calls but leaves it to the official umpire to actually make the umpiring calls. Alternatively, the buddy or the teacher can provide quiet, ongoing feedback on how well the umpire is doing. The buddy umpire system also raises the issue of how difficult officiating can be (for example, making a decision, calling it out and dealing with player reactions—both when they agree and disagree with the call) and provides a wonderful opportunity for further class discussions especially around umpire roles and fair play.

Understanding of Tactics and Strategies

The questions regarding tactics and strategies in form 5.1 relate quite generically to team invasion games. They concern maintaining possession, moving into space and defensive concepts. You can apply these questions to many of the non-specific games within this text as well as to specific sports. If you can get your students to both respond correctly and try to implement this tactical knowledge, then you will have achieved much in developing their tactical knowledge.

While questions relating to rules typically have only one correct answer, when it comes to tactical questions you can have responses that demonstrate various degrees of correctness. Rather than have one correct answer you might allocate different point values to answers. In discussion with students, you could point out that tactical responses typically relate to basic principles and game scenarios often provide more than one way in relation to those principles of achieving the desired outcome.

When you review the student responses to questions on tactics, you will see gaps in their tactical knowledge. Armed with this feedback, you will have an opportunity to fill in those gaps either within the immediate activity or game you are playing or at a later date, when applying the same tactical concept in another activity.

If you design your own activities or games to teach tactical knowledge, keep them simple but ensure they replicate the shape or tactical principles associated with the actual game.

For example, let's say you want to reinforce the game strategy of maintaining possession of a ball. Your students are playing a game of 5v3 football. The numerical superiority of the team of five should enable players on that team to maintain

Field Hockey Survey

Name: _____   Class: _____

Playing Background: Please tick the description that best describes you in relation to the game of hockey.

1. I have never played.
2. I play at school or at home with my friends.
3. I used to play for a club team on Saturdays.
4. I am currently a member of a hockey team.

Understanding of Basic Rules: Circle the answer you think is correct.

1. To start the game of hockey, you may pass or dribble the ball
   - forward or backwards
   - only backwards
   - only sideways
2. At the start of a game of hockey,
   - all players must be in their own defensive half
   - all players must be in their own defensive back third
   - players may be in any part of the field
3. After a goal has been scored, the team just scored against restarts the game with a pass or dribble from
   - in front of its goal
   - anywhere in its half
   - in the middle at the halfway point
4. If the ball goes out over the sideline, the game is restarted when the ball is
   - passed or dribbled into play from where it went out
   - passed or dribbled into play from anywhere behind where it went out
   - passed or dribbled into play anywhere along the side where it went out

Understanding of Tactics and Strategies: Circle the answer you think is correct.

1. When your team has the ball on attack, it is best to
   - spread out
   - bunch up
   - stay beside the person with the ball
2. When your team has the ball, a good tactic is to
   - always go forward towards the opponent's goal
   - try to go forward but sometimes use back or side passes if it is difficult to go forward
   - always pass the ball forward because one of your players might get the ball and score a goal
3. As a general idea for marking opponents in hockey, you should stand
   - in front of your opponent
   - beside your opponent
   - between your opponent and your goal

FORM 5.1   Sample authentic assessment form.

4. When one player in your team marks one player in the opposing team, that is called

- close marking
- man-to-man marking
- even marking

5. When you are defending and your team spreads out and marks an area in front of your goal, that type of defence is called

- zone defence
- team defence
- group defence

6. To help your team-mates make good passes, you should

- stand still and call out to them so they know where you are
- run slowly into spaces to receive a pass
- dodge or use a quick sprint into space to receive a pass

7. After you pass the ball to a team-mate, you should

- stand still and watch to see if your team-mate receives the ball
- call out to your team-mate and encourage him to get to your pass
- move to a new space on the field in case your team-mate wants to pass the ball back to you

Affective Learning: To answer the next questions, either circle the words that best describe how you feel or put a tick on the line closest to the answer you like the best.

1. I will enjoy playing hockey.
- Disagree strongly
- Disagree somewhat
- Agree somewhat
- Agree strongly

2. I know the rules of hockey.
- Disagree strongly
- Disagree somewhat
- Agree somewhat
- Agree strongly

3. I understand hockey tactics.
- Disagree strongly
- Disagree somewhat
- Agree somewhat
- Agree strongly

4. I think I will be able to help my team when playing in the hockey lessons.
- Disagree strongly
- Disagree somewhat
- Agree somewhat
- Agree strongly

Note: The post-instruction survey would need to be written in the past tense.

FORM 5.1   Sample authentic assessment form. (*continued*)

possession of the ball if they use back and around passes. To ensure that this happens, establish the following modification regarding throwing the ball back into play. If the person throwing in opts to throw the ball back towards her defensive area, the receiver of the throw is allowed a free trap of the ball (i.e., the opposition cannot tackle her until the ball is under control). This rule does not take away the tactic of throwing forward, that is a tactical decision the person throwing the ball in has to make, but it reinforces the possession concept of a simple possession back pass rather than risk the forward pass that might result in turning the ball over to the opposition.

Affective Learning

This section of the questionnaire can provide valuable insights into students' enjoyment and understanding of the game (or lack thereof). Repeating this survey after the lesson can give you extremely valuable insights into whether your class or team's level of enjoyment and self-confidence has increased. It has been my experience that using modifying games and teaching from a tactical perspective gives players an opportunity to gain enjoyment from contributing to the team performance that traditional game learning experiences do not always allow and increases the chances of student affective outcomes being positive.

ASSESSING TEAM PERFORMANCE

After diagnosing players' knowledge of and feelings towards activities, you can move on to assessing qualities related to their team performance: cooperative behaviour, decision making and technique.

Cooperative Behaviour

A star team will always beat a team of stars! Although I cannot recall who originally coined this oft-quoted phrase, the message for those who play team games is quite explicit: If you subjugate your own interests and cooperate in favour of the team, you will beat a team of stars who do not cooperate and play as individuals.

The procedures used to assess cooperative game play, and the associated feedback to players, are designed to improve individual contributions and team performance. In addition, such an assessment can also help you with class, or group, management.

Assessing cooperative behaviour is best undertaken as formative assessment while the lessons are still in progress. Players should be taught the need for cooperative play and what that means in terms of on-field performance. They should then be given opportunities to discuss the feedback they receive.

It is important to involve the players in the process of determining the criteria by which their level of cooperative play will be assessed. In mutual discussions, help them understand and accept the outcomes you have in mind, rather than arbitrarily asserting them. If the players believe they have input into the assessment process, they will be more likely to experience ownership of the desired behaviour. In this way they will be working for themselves and the team and not just towards a goal you have established.

Consider the following examples of cooperative assessment criteria. (*Note: On-ball attacking* and *off-ball attacking support* refer to when the player or his team has possession of the ball. *On-ball defending* and *off-ball defensive support* refer to when the player's team does not have possession of the ball.)

- *Off-ball attacking support:* The player does not have the ball but moves into space to support attacking play.
- *Off-ball defensive support:* The player is not directly confronting the opponent in possession of the ball but is providing defensive support following a turnover of possession.
- *Positive verbal feedback to team-mates:* The player calls out in support of good play, a team-mate's attempt to play well or obvious effort by team-mates.

Form 5.2 shows a sample form to illustrate the kind of assessment you could use with players to evaluate cooperative play. The following scenario relates to the assessment form. You can assign a team member to fill in the assessment as part of learning about cooperative game play. First, teach the players the meaning of the established criteria. Then, assign five players per team but have them play 4v4. The fifth person on each team is assigned to fill in the assessment form as part of learning about cooperative game play. She undertakes this pencil-and-paper game analysis for a set period (e.g., five minutes). She watches one player and records the number of times she observes the specified behaviour in five minutes. After five minutes, the observed player switches roles with the observer and assesses another player.

Cooperative Team Play

Assessor: _____   Player: _____

In this sample form, each time the observer sees opportunities for a cooperative attribute, he or she places a tick in the column beside that attribute. This provides the total number of trials for that activity.

In this example, for off-ball attacking support the observer noted 8 opportunities for the player to demonstrate that quality, which the player did on 7 of those occasions. Of the 6 opportunities to provide off-ball defensive support, the player responded positively 3 times. The assessor heard the player give positive feedback only once.

The results are then converted to a percentage and placed in a column indicating whether that aspect needs work (to improve), is developing or is good. The assessed player then has an opportunity to respond to the feedback.

Cooperative attribute	Number of trials	Needs work (<50%)	Developing (50-70%)	Good (>70%)
Off-ball attacking support	/ / / / / / x /			✓
Off-ball defensive Support	/ / / x x x		✓	
Positive verbal feedback to team-mates during game	/	✓		

1. I think this feedback is . . .

Fair and quite accurate. I think I should have done more defensive work, but we were winning the game comfortably and so I guess I got a little lazy. I definitely need to say more!

2. My individual goal is to . . .

Provide more verbal support to the team.

3. The agreed goal to improve team performance is to . . .

Improve our support in defence and talk more in support of each other's efforts, especially in off-ball play.

FORM 5.2 Sample form for assessing cooperative play.

After all players have been assessed, have them look at their assessments (game analysis sheets) and make brief comments on them. Based on their analysis of the feedback, individual players set goals for improving one or more aspects of their cooperative play. Team members may also discuss together where they might best improve their team performance by concentrating on an area for improvement.

Before undertaking this type of formative assessment, players need to be taught what to look for. To do this, you need to teach them about the value of cooperative team play to ensure that they are fair in their assessments of their peers. The assessment requires keen observation techniques, and to do this form of assessment well, players need to keep developing their understanding of the game.

The benefits of this type of assessment do not accrue only to the player being assessed. To make valid comments about their team-mates, assessors must understand the nature of cooperative play and how it contributes to team performance. Explain to assessors the value of this type of assessment and its function in developing their own understanding and performance in games. It is my experience that the assessors are often encouraged to either include or eliminate aspects of play they observe in other team members immediately after they return to the game.

Although not primarily developed for this purpose, this type of assessment and the resulting feedback give you a wonderful management tool. With a player who is not making much of an effort, rather than exhorting him to greater effort for your sake, you could review his assessment card and say something like the following (the purpose of my emphasis of *you* and *your* is to point out the importance of emphasising the player; I would not verbally emphasise these words with the player):

> I see that *you* listed as *your* goal to provide more positive feedback to *your* team-mates, and that the team goal that *you* helped select was to work harder off the ball defensively. Perhaps *you* can explain why *you* set those goals and yet I cannot see any evidence of *your* doing what *you* said *you* would do?

Giving ownership of the desired behaviour to the player changes the nature of the management episode. You are not asking the player to exhibit the behaviour because you want him to; *he* chose it as a goal. If *he* set a goal to play in a manner that

helps his team, what is preventing that outcome? In effect, the player has to explain why he is not doing what he set as a goal behaviour. He cannot justify resenting or blaming you (in theory), because you did not choose the game behaviour.

Decision Making and Technique

Earlier in this text, I mentioned that an authentic definition of skill in games was not just technique but Alan Launder's (2003) description of skill in games that states skill equals tactics plus technique. Tactics are employed after some thought and decision making but they also usually require good game skill techniques to execute them. The components are of course inseparable, in most sports. Because they are inseparable one can often assess them within games simultaneously. The key to this within-game authentic player decision-making and technique assessment is in establishing the criteria against which performance and performers will be measured. Although establishing the decision-making and technique criteria is quite difficult, doing so is extremely important for providing useful feedback for the players and teacher. Because of the difficulty of establishing this criteria, you may have to take a greater role in leading your students to the assessment criteria, but you still want to avoid arbitrarily imposing the criteria on the students.

Establishing criteria for technique assessment may require you to demonstrate to students the correct technique. If you cannot demonstrate yourself and you have no visual model (e.g., video), you may want to have a student who can perform the desired technique at or close to the level you require, demonstrate it to the class or group. You can then lead the rest of the class to agree that the student's performance is the desired technical outcome. It could be argued that assessing technique is reverting to a traditional game learning approach and that you could run the risk of alienating those students for whom the TGfU approach is hoping to provide positive inclusive outcomes. The following provides a way of avoiding this:

- Establish small, incremental mastery standards that lead students towards mastery of the desired technique. The base level of mastery performance you establish should allow for basic execution of the technique and an opportunity for students to participate in a game at their level of expertise with enjoyment.

- Provide modified assessment games that allow the players trying to master or perform the technique plenty of time to do so. This can be achieved through modified rules or simply by giving a team a numerical advantage (e.g., 5v3). The imbalance in team numbers provides time and less pressure for the players to execute the technique within the context of a game. As techniques improve, you can adjust the numbers per team to place the players under greater pressure to perform the technique and engage in more complex decision making.

Consider the following modified game of football as an example of decision-making and technique assessment criteria. (In this example, it is assumed that players already have quite well developed basic techniques in the game. In this modified game there are seven players per team.)

Outcomes and Assessment Focus

Technique Outcomes

- Passing and dribbling
- Crossing the ball into the goal box area
- Offensive and defensive heading
- Defending and attacking from lofted passes
- For goalkeepers, catching the lofted pass

Decision Making Outcomes

For the goal keeper, deciding whether to move to try to intercept and catch the lofted centre pass.

Strategic Outcomes

To understand the value of playing wide

Set up a modified football game with three field players, two wide attackers (channel players), one goalkeeper and one assessor per team (see figure 5.1). The channel players play outside of the field in left- and right-side channels that run the length of the playing area. The assessor needs a clipboard, pencil and marking table. Rotate positions so all players experience the various roles in the game.

Note: Some players may not see themselves as goalkeepers, but all players, especially young ones, should experience all of the positions to develop their understanding of the game.

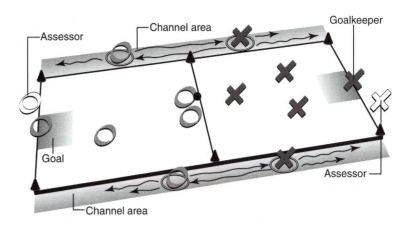

FIGURE 5.1 Modified football game set-up.

The field players play a normal 3v3 game of football but should be encouraged to use the tactic of playing wide by using either of their left- or right-side channel players for outlet passes. The channel players cannot be tackled by any member of the opposition and should, for the purposes of this game, be encouraged to dribble the ball down their side and then centre the ball, in the air, into the goal box in front of the opponents' goal.

The object of the game is, of course, to score goals. The modification of the use of channel players does not impede that outcome, but it does make the likelihood of having the ball lofted into the goal box area much greater than if the game were more conventional. The change also allows for more opportunities to assess the performance of the goalies in reasonably authentic conditions.

Assessment Procedure

It takes only a short time to explain the performance criteria. Set up the game and assign one player from each team to undertake the assessor role. Have players play the game for a set time (e.g., 5 minutes); then stop the game and give time for the assessed player to see and hear his feedback from the assessor. After getting feedback, players rotate positions, including being the assessor and repeat the game.

The students who want to play a game are satisfied, but you are doing far more than merely facilitating an unstructured game. You are teaching a basic strategy, targeting specific attacking and defensive skills and using an authentic assessment tool to give the players a deeper insight into the nature of games.

Form 5.3 is a form for assessing the goalkeeper's decision to try to intercept the centred ball by

Goalkeeping Assessment Form

Assessor: _____   Goalkeeper: _____

Assessors: Carefully observe your goalkeeper. Place a tick or cross in the appropriate column based on your observations of their decision making and movement techniques.

Performance criteria: The goalkeeper tries to intercept and catch the centred ball.

Decision making: Appropriate: Goalkeeper intercepts the ball (i.e., touches it)

Inappropriate: Goalkeeper tries for the interception but does not touch the ball

Technique Performance: Successful: Goalkeeper successfully catches the ball

Unsuccessful: Goalkeeper touches but does not gain control of the ball

Trials	DECISION MAKING		TECHNIQUE PERFORMANCE	
	Appropriate (gets to and touches the ball)	Inappropriate (does not get to the ball)	Successful (gets to and catches the ball)	Unsuccessful (gets to but does not gain control of the ball)
1				
2				
3				
4				
Total				
Ratio				

Reflective comments by goalkeeper:

FORM 5.3   Sample form for assessing a goalkeeper's decision making and movement technique.

catching it and his performance of that task. If you were using this form, you would instruct the assessors to carefully observe the goalkeeper and place a tick or cross in the appropriate column based on the goalkeeper's decision making and performance of the set task.

CONCLUSION

Authentic assessment is not intrusive of game instruction and does not lead to the inevitable questions of, Do we have to do this assessment? When are we going to have a game? This is because an authentic game context is central to the assessment process. Although I have confined the assessment examples in this chapter to pencil and paper, there are obvious opportunities to use technology, especially video recording and digital photography. This would allow you to include technology outcomes in your lesson planning and has the potential to capture the interest of even more students than the traditional core of students who tend to love games no matter what they are doing.

To state that playing team games is a social experience is stating the obvious. In fact, the social nature and supposed character-developing qualities of games (e.g., teamwork, cooperation, discipline, accepting the good with the bad and self-sacrifice) have long been trumpeted as the raison d'être for the inclusion of games within schooling. Teamwork is applauded as a good that can come from playing games. Despite the obvious social and team dimensions of games, motor skill researchers and physical education teachers have focused on individual development as a measure of learning in games (Griffin & Placek, 2001). This has led to instruction (frequently referred to as a traditional approach) that has focused on individual technique, largely ignoring those qualities that provided the rationale for the inclusion of

game instruction in physical education contexts in the first place.

Traditional assessment and subsequent instruction has also ignored the conditions within games that require social interaction and qualities associated with teamwork—namely, that games are associated with tactics and strategies. It appears obvious to state that an understanding of the tactics of offence and defence in games is a necessary condition for successful play.

Advocacy of an authentic approach to assessment in this text reflects my belief about the social interaction and cooperative nature of successful game play. Rovegno, Nevett, Brock and Babiarz (2001), in an investigation into learning in games, coined a phrase: 'throwing the catchable pass' (p. 374). The term highlights both the community and team nature of game play. First, the player with the ball has to know the recipient of the pass in terms of what that player can catch. It is not a question of simply choosing from long-term memory a generalised motor programme of an overarm throw and executing it. The passer has to take into account the context of the game, the environment and the abilities of the receiver. If an outcome for improving performance in a game is to improve the number of passes caught by the team, then the assessment must also focus on the reciprocal nature of the catchable pass.

Assessing performance during game play in this manner provides a whole new dimension for teaching and assessment. Authentic assessment overcomes concerns about not having enough time to both teach and assess game play by building assessment into the game experience. Finally, it requires you to think holistically about what you want students to learn about game play, which changes what and how you teach and in turn makes your and your students' experiences so much more interesting, educative and enjoyable than they would be using a traditional skills-based approach to instruction and assessment.

Glossary

Although some of the terms used in this book are well known and self-explanatory, the following provides general definitions.

agility—The ability to move very quickly and with ease, including changes of direction and sometimes in height or position (e.g., dodging, sliding on the surface, getting quickly up onto one's feet and moving in another direction).

anticipation—The ability to visualize a future event based on past experience and clues picked up from another player's action; gives players the capacity to decide how to respond before the event transpires.

back and around pass—Taking a ball out of one area and moving it back and around (away from the opposition) before launching another attack, usually on the other side of the court or field.

blocking—Deliberately but legally stepping between an attacker and a defender to prevent the defender from either getting at the ball carrier or intercepting a pass; also known as screening.

body language—The use of body cues to communicate to team-mates an intended action (e.g., a hand or eye movement to signal direction).

caught square—When two defenders change their covering roles and momentarily are in a straight line (i.e., square).

channeling—Delaying a tackle on an attacker in order to direct him in a particular direction (e.g., towards the sideline or another defender).

communication—Using talking and body language to keep everyone in the team aware of what is happening. It is especially important when leading, or in defence when playing games that allow the attack to operate behind the defence. It is also important in marking; Players can call team-mates onto, or make them aware of, unmarked players.

congesting space—Placing defenders in such a way that attackers have reduced space or time in which to work or make decisions.

counter-attack—The movement, usually very quickly, from defence to attack across the field or court.

covering—Marking that provides layers of defence. It usually involves one player confronting the opposition and the other covering the possible passing option.

depth—Longitudinal forward and backward space in a game. Depth can be used in offensive or defensive strategies or team formations.

disguise—The act of hiding one's true intentions (e.g., looking one way and passing another way).

double-teaming—A situation in which two defenders mark or tackle one attacker.

draw and pass—A situation in which the on-ball attacker runs at (targets) a defender, drawing him towards him and, just before he would be tackled, passes the ball to a support player.

elimination game—In minor games or drills, an activity that typically removes players from participation when they fail at the technique (e.g., drop the ball or are tagged). Elimination games are generally considered counterproductive to learning.

emptying the space—Dodging out of the area in which one wants to receive the ball to draw the opposition marker away and then dodging back into it once it is empty.

fast break—A very fast counter-attack, moving from defence to attack as quickly as possible. In ball games such as basketball, this is typically done with a long outlet pass.

feint—The act of pretending to move one way or do one thing and moving another way or doing something other than indicated.

half-court defence—A form of defence in which a team retreats into its half and starts to defend only when the opposition has advanced over halfway.

invasion game—A game in which players or teams defend territory and have to invade the opposition's territory to score points (e.g., football, rugby).

isolating—Restricting the movement or passing options of an attacker (e.g., marking all of her possible passing options or channeling her away from support players).

layering in defence—A progressive defensive system that commits more and more players to the defensive role as the opposition's attack nears the team's main defensive zone.

leading—Moving into space without the ball in an effort to provide a possible pass option, draw defenders out of set positions or provide more options for the ball carrier.

man-to-man marking—A system of defence in which each defender marks one player. Players often swap whom they're marking, but every attacker must be marked by a defender.

match-ups and mismatches—The pairing of players with the opposition either as equals (match-ups) or unequals (mismatches).

net game—Any game where a net is used to divide the playing area (e.g., tennis and badminton).

off-ball attacking support—Any player in your team who does not have the ball but moves into space to support the attacking play of the on-ball attacking player.

off-ball defensive support—Any player in your team who is not directly confronting the opponent in possession of the ball but is providing defensive support to your player who is directly confronting the opponent's on-ball attacker.

on-ball attacker—The attacker in possession of the ball.

on-ball defender—The player directly confronting the opposition player in possession of the ball.

one-two pass—A quick interchange of passes between two players.

picking up a player—Usually refers to a defensive call to a defender to mark a player who is currently not being marked.

pivot—Keeping one foot grounded and spinning on that foot to change the position of the other foot. A pivot is restricted to one step.

rotation—Moving players into and out of a game; also called substitution.

set-play—A rehearsed move that takes place in an open-skill game (e.g., a throw-in or free kick in football or a penalty corner in hockey).

sliding defence—Defending inside attackers in a way that doesn't confront them but forces them to move wide eventually constricting the space in which the final player to receive the ball has to move.

space—An area that is uncontested or not marked by the opposition. Room in which the player is free to move without close marking from the opposition. Also associated with time.

split—When two players start together and then move rapidly apart making it difficult for one opposing player to mark them.

target game—A game in which the object is to hit a target (e.g., archery, golf).

team cooperation—Unselfish play by players who work at providing opportunities for team-mates.

triangle marking—Marking behind or slightly in front and off to one side of a possible receiver. The lines between the two attackers and the defender form the triangle.

V-leading—When an off-ball attacking player leads back towards and then quickly away from the on-ball attacker to escape a defender. The sudden dodge and change in direction is undertaken to find space and provide a passing option for the on-ball attacker.

wall game—A game in which players use a wall to rebound an object (e.g., squash).

width—Playing width. A game strategy that involves having players playing as wide as possible on the pitch or field. In some games such players are called 'wings' (e.g., field hockey, rugby).

zone defence—A system of defence in which defenders mark an area or space rather than a specific person.

Bibliography

Bunker, D.J. (1982). Taking an understanding approach to the teaching of cricket: An example of a fielding game. *Bulletin of PE,* 19 (1).

Bunker, D.J., & Thorpe, R.D. (1982). A model for teaching games in secondary schools. *Bulletin of PE,* 18 (1).

den Duyn, N. (1996). Why it makes sense to play games. *Sports Coach.* 19 (3), 6-9.

den Duyn, N. (1997). Games sense: It's time to play. *Sports Coach.* 19 (4), 3-8.

Griffin, L.L., & Butler, J.L. (2005). *Teaching games for understanding: Theory, research and practice.* Champaign, IL: Human Kinetics.

Griffin, L.L., & Placek, J.H. (2001). The understanding and development of learners' domain-specific knowledge: Concluding comments. *Journal of Teaching in Physical Education,* 20 (4), 402-406.

Holt, N.L., Strean, W.B., & Bengoechea, E.G. (2002). Expanding the Teaching Games for Understanding model: New avenues for future research and practice. *Journal of Teaching in Physical Education,* 21 (2), 162-176.

Hooper, T. (2003). Four R's for tactical awareness: Applying game performance assessment in net/wall game. *Journal of Teaching Elementary Physical Education,* 4(2), 16-21.

Kidman, L. (2001). *Developing decision makers: An empowerment approach to coaching.* New Zealand: Innovative Print Communications. See especially chapter 2, by Rod Thorpe on Teaching Games for Understanding.

Kirk, D., & MacPhail, A. (2002). Teaching Games for Understanding and situated learning: Rethinking the Bunker-Thorpe model. *Journal of Teaching in Physical Education,* 21 (2), 177-192.

Launder, A.G. (2001). *Play practice: A games approach to teaching and coaching sport.* Champaign, IL: Human Kinetics.

Launder, A.G. (2003). Revisit 'game sense.' *Sports Coach,* 26 (1), 32-34.

Lave, J., & Wenger, E. (1991). *Situated learning: Legitimate peripheral participation.* Cambridge, UK: Cambridge University Press.

Light, R. (2003). The joy of learning: Emotion and learning in games through TGfU. *Journal of Physical Education New Zealand,* 36 (1), 93-108.

Light, R., & Georgakis, S. (2005). Integrating theory and practice in teacher education: The impact of a game sense unit on female pre-service primary teachers' attitudes towards teaching physical education. *Journal of Physical Education New Zealand,* 38 (1), 67-80.

Mosston, M. (1992). Tug-o-war, no more: Meeting teaching and learning objectives using the spectrum of teaching styles. *Journal of Physical Education & Dance,* 63 (1), 27-31.

Pope, C.C. (2005). Once more with feeling: Rethinking and playing with the Teaching Games for Understanding model. *Journal of Physical Education and Sport Pedagogy,* 10 (3), 271-286.

Pope, C.C. (2006). Affect in New Zealand junior sport: The forgotten dynamic. *Change: Transformation Education,* 9 (1), 17-26.

Rink, J. (2001). Investigating the assumptions of pedagogy. *Journal of Teaching in Physical Education,* 20 (2), 112-128.

Rink, J., French, K., Werner, P., Lynn, S., & Mays, A. (1992). The influence of content development on the effectiveness of instruction. *Journal of Teaching in Physical Education,* 11, 139-149.

Rovegno, I., Nevett, M., Brock, S., & Babiarz, M. (2001). Teaching and learning basic invasion-game tactics in 4th grade: A descriptive study from situated and constraints theoretical perspectives. *Journal of Teaching in Physical Education,* 20 (4), 370-388.

Sanders, L., & Kidman, L. (1998, Summer). Can primary school children perform fundamental motor-skills? *Journal of Physical Education New Zealand,* 31 (4), 11-13.

Schmidt, R., & Wrisberg, C.A. (2004) *Motor learning and performance: A problem-based learning approach* (3rd ed.). Champaign, IL: Human Kinetics.

Siedentop, D., Mand, C., & Taggart, A. (1986). Sports education. In *Physical education: Teaching and curriculum strategies for grades 5-12.* Palo Alto, CA: Mayfield.

Slade, D.G. (2003). *Stick2hockey.* Palmerston North, New Zealand: Stick2hockey Publishing Limited.

Slade, D.G. (2005). *Teaching attack and defence in team games: A TGfU approach.* Palmerston North, New Zealand: Stick2hockey Publishing Limited.

Slade, D.G. (2007). Making first coaching impressions count through a Teaching Games for Understanding approach. *Sports Coach,* 29 (4), 28-29.

Sport and Recreation New Zealand. (2006, March 30). Participation in sport & active leisure by NZ 5-8 year olds. Available: www.sparc.org.nz/research-policy/research/participation/participation-5-8-year-olds.

Sport and Recreation New Zealand. (2006, March 30). Participation in sport & active leisure by NZ 9-12 year olds. Available: www.sparc.org.nz/research-policy/research/participation/participation-9-12-year-olds.

Styles, L. (Ed.). (1974). *Theories for teaching*. New York: Dodd, Mead, & Co.

Sweeting, T., & Rink, J. (1999). Effects of direct instruction and environmentally designed instruction on the process and product characteristics of a fundamental skill. *Journal of Teaching in Physical Education*, 18 (2), 216-233.

Thorpe, R.D. (1982, Spring). An understanding approach to the teaching of tennis. *Bulletin of PE*, 19 (1), 24-28.

Thorpe, R.D., & Bunker, D.J. (1982, Spring). From theory to practice: Two examples of an understanding approach to the teaching of games. *Bulletin of PE*, 18 (1).

Thorpe, R.D., & Bunker, D.J. (1982, Spring). Issues that arise when preparing to teach for understanding. *Bulletin of PE*, 19 (1).

Turner, A., & Martineck, T. (1995). Teaching for Understanding. A model for improving decision making during game play. *Quest*, 47, 4-63.

Werner, P. (1989, March). Teaching games: A tactical perspective. *Journal of Teaching in Physical Education*, 97-101.

Werner, P., & Almond, L. (1990, April). Models of games education. *Journal of Physical Education Recreation & Dance*.

Werner, P., Thorpe, R.D., & Bunker, D. (1996). Teaching Games for Understanding: Evolution of a model. *Journal of Teaching in Physical Education*, 67 (1), 28-33.

Index

Note: Page numbers followed by an italicized *f* or t indicate a figure or table is on that page, respectively.

About the Author

Dennis G. Slade, MPhil, is a senior lecturer and coordinator of the BEd secondary physical education degree at Massey University in Palmerston North, New Zealand. He has played national and international sport and is currently a member of the New Zealand men's masters field hockey team. He has had a long career in teaching physical education and coaching sport and was the head coach of the New Zealand U16 boys' field hockey academy. Dennis is the author of *Senior School Physical Education: A Course Book for New Zealand Schools* (two editions), *Teaching Attack and Defence in Team Games: A TGfU Approach* (5 reprints) and a CD-ROM *Stick2hockey,* a TGfU approach to teaching field hockey to novices. He has presented at two international TGfU conferences, was the keynote presenter for the West Zone Physical Education Conference in Singapore (2006) and has presented numerous workshops on TGfU and game sense approaches to game instruction in New Zealand. His research interests include youth and masters sport, the TGfU and game sense methodologies, and physical activity.

You'll find other outstanding
physical education resources at
www.HumanKinetics.com